T*SQ Transgender Studies Quarterly

Volume 6 ∗ Number 2 ∗ May 2019

Trans Studies en las Américas

Edited by Claudia Sofía Garriga-López, Denilson Lopes,
Cole Rizki, and Juana María Rodríguez

ARTS & CULTURE

BOOK REVIEW

General Editor's Introduction

FRANCISCO J. GALARTE

The publication of this special issue, "Trans Studies en las Américas," marks the start of my tenure as general coeditor of *TSQ*. It is an honor to replace Paisley Currah as general coeditor and to work alongside my colleague Susan Stryker to further cultivate the originality, innovation, irreverence, and disruption that marks the scholarship published within the only interdisciplinary journal for trans cultural studies. As the only trans scholar of color who is a part of the Transgender Studies Research Cluster at the University of Arizona, I felt it was especially pressing to accept the invitation from Susan and Paisley to transition from my role as fashion editor and editorial board member to general coeditor. My own scholarship finds its home in trans studies, Latina/o/x studies, and Chicana/o/x studies, so serving as the overseeing general coeditor for this issue felt especially serendipitous. As noted by Cole Rizki in the special issue introduction, this issue of *TSQ* was born out of a series of panels at International Trans Studies*: An International Transdisciplinary Conference on Gender, Embodiment, and Sexuality at the University of Arizona in 2016. The transhemispheric reach of the issue, with its record number of submissions, spanning three languages, is an indicator that further publication opportunities are necessary for trans and Latin/x American and Caribbean studies scholarship. This issue is only the beginning, as the question of the *x* in Latina/o and Latin American studies continues to take shape.

The editors of this issue propose the term *Latin/x America* to account for the incoherence and "entanglements of 'US' and 'Latin America' as geopolitical categories." Perhaps most important, noted by Rizki in the special issue introduction, is the institutional precarity of trans studies in the Global South. While in the Global North trans studies' institutionalization has resulted in the creation of faculty cluster hires, individual faculty positions, and research positions, many do not emphasize scholarship focused on Latinx or Latin America. By the same token, it is rare for Latinx and Latin American studies positions to emphasize scholarship focused on trans studies. The slash used by the coeditors of this volume to split *Latin/x* is a cut that implores us to consider why trans studies in *las Américas*? The essays, archival materials, narratives, and cultural productions in this issue overwhelmingly let us know why and how trans studies in a Latin/x American context is timely and urgent. The overwhelming response to the call for papers for this issue also announces that this platform is not enough.

In a special issue of the journal of the American Studies Association, *American Quarterly*, titled "Las Américas Quarterly," its coeditors, Macarena Gómez-Barris and Licia Fiol-Matta (2014: 504), describe the *x* as "a turn away from the dichotomous, toward a void, an unknown, a wrestling with plurality, vectors of multi-intentionality, and the transitional meanings of what has yet to be seen." This *TSQ* special issue, "Trans Studies en las Américas," cuts through the void, confronts the unknown, and highlights the plurality and *transitional* meanings gestured to by Gómez-Barris and Fiol-Matta. The special issue editors raise the stakes by introducing a "*travesti*-trans analytic" mode of inquiry marked by the potentiality of bringing "existing Latin/x American subjectivities, activist strategies, and theories . . . into conversation with US-oriented trans studies." This analytic highlights how *trans-* (embodiment, mobility, sexuality, corporeality, politics, lexicons) informs site-specific micropolitical networks of social resistance in *las Américas* that "unyieldingly reappropriate and intervene in the advocacy slogans of 'woman,' 'identity,' 'liberty' or 'equality,' in other words, to disseminate 'living revolutions'" (Valencia 2018: 263, quoting Preciado 2009: 59).[1] Inspired in part by Félix Guattari's writings on molecular politics, Paul Preciado's "living revolutions" focuses on the flows, becomings, transitions between phases, and intensities of a molecular order.

A focus on the molecular order allows us to see "trans-" and "Latin/x America" as categories that index "the impasse of pure verticality and that of mere horizontality," for example, to consider the verticality implied in global "north" and "south" and the horizontality within the "across" of the prefixial *trans-* (Guattari 1984: 18). Thus, a way to confront this impasse is a turn to Guattari's transversality as a dimension that requires "maximum communication among different levels and, above all, in different meanings" (18). The result might then be realized as *travesti*-trans, a mode of intervention and transformation that "enable[s] us to conceive of alliances and systems of transversality" (Guattari and Rolnik 2007: 265). In the book *Molecular Revolution in Brazil*, Guattari and Suely Rolnik (2007: 261) assert that revolution "is the whole range of possibilities of specific practices of change in the way of life, with their creative potential, that constitutes what I call molecular revolution, which is a condition for any social transformation." The context for this statement is an atmosphere of the reactivation of public life amid the first direct elections after nearly two decades of military dictatorship in Brazil in 1982. They describe this period as one of "productivity, proliferation, creation, utterly fabulous revolutions" (9). From this viewpoint Guattari and Rolnik observe a "multiple people, a people of mutants, a people of potentialities that appears and disappears," a silent molecular revolution propelled by the force of "what was happening in the politics of desire, of subjectivity, of relationship with the other" (9). The vitality, potentiality, becoming that mark that moment resonate contemporarily in the affective charge present in the various modes through which "living revolutions" intervene within discourse from the various scales of life and the multiple locales represented in this special issue.

In 2018, nearly thirty-six years after Guattari's observations on molecular revolution and amid the current swerve of the right we are seeing the ascension of Trump in the United States, Brexit in Europe, and most recently, the election of Jair Bolsonaro in Brazil. Of most resonance is the threat that Bolsonaro's election could mean a return to a military dictatorship and threaten the rights of women, LGBT folks, and people of color (Londoño and Darlington 2018). As Guattari and Rolnik teach us in *Molecular Revolution in Brazil* (2007: 9), a micropolitical change independent of the state's direction provides the opportunity to examine the degree to which theoretical and strategic issues formulated by the "multiple people, people of mutants, people of potentialities" may give way to new movements. This is to say, if revolution is a "certain moment of *trans*formation . . . a moment of irreversibility in a process" (259), then the whole range of *travesti*-trans interventions being made across *las Américas* that teem with creativity, refusal, and vitality in the face of precarity are anything but utopian or idealistic; they set the stage for myriad forms of social transformation.

"Trans Studies en las Américas," then, implores us to consider, and with urgency, what sorts of micropolitical alliances and embodied forms of resistance might be possible between US-oriented trans studies and Latin/x American *travesti*-trans forms of knowledge production.

Francisco J. Galarte is assistant professor of gender and women's studies at the University of Arizona, where he teaches Chicana/Latina studies and transgender studies.

Note

1.   "Reapropiación e intervención irreductibles a los slogans de defensa de la 'mujer,' la 'identidad,' la 'libertad,' o la 'igualdad,' es decir, poner en común 'revoluciones vivas.'"

References

Gómez-Barris, Macarena, and Licia Fiol-Matta. 2014. Introduction to "Las Américas Quarterly," edited by Macarena Gómez-Barris and Licia Fiol-Matta. Special issue, *American Quarterly* 66, no. 3: 493–505.

Guattari, Félix. 1984. *Molecular Revolution: Psychiatry and Politics.* New York: Penguin.

Guattari, Félix, and Suely Rolnik. 2007. *Molecular Revolution in Brazil.* Translated by Karel Clapshow and Brian Holmes. Cambridge, MA: MIT Press.

Londoño, Ernesto, and Shasta Darlington. 2018. "Far-Right Candidate Jair Bolsonaro Widens Lead in Brazil's Presidential Race." *New York Times*, October 5. www.nytimes.com/2018/10/05/world/americas/brazil-presidential-race-bolsonaro.html.

Preciado, Paul. 2009. "Transfeminismos y micropolíticas del género en la era farmaco pornográfica." *Revista Artecontexto*, May. www.artecontexto.com/es/leer_en_linea-21.html.

Valencia, Sayak. 2018. *Gore Capitalism.* Translated by John Pluecker. Cambridge, MA: MIT Press.

Latin/x American Trans Studies
Toward a Travesti-*Trans Analytic*

COLE RIZKI

Travesti activist Lohana Berkins stands in the foreground, her fist raised in struggle and solidarity (fig. 1). Behind a wave of blood red fabric, a swell of protestors chant, lifting pink and blue signs high above their heads demanding *justicia* for Diana Sacayán. The hand-painted word *compañera* peeks out from the fabric's folds, curling across the collective's banner in bold, black cursive outlined in soft baby blue. *Compañera*—a word thick with complicity, friendship, solidarity, and struggle—manifests the crowd's affective commitments. The banner enfolds the march in a loose, sensuous weave as protestors flood the streets of Buenos Aires denouncing Diana's murder.

One sign in the upper right-hand corner stands out from the rest: painted in black, Diana Sacayán's portrait overlays the pan-indigenous *wiphala* flag's checkered pattern, framed by the words *trava sudaca originaria*. Diana's singular self-identification defies easy translation, and yet the phrase condenses many of the central concerns of "Trans Studies en las Américas": the geopolitics of *travesti* and trans representation practices, political alliances, and demands for bodily sovereignty inflected by legal forms, human rights discourses, racial formations, and indigenous territorial claims. These concerns, which exceed sexed and gendered identification, are variously contoured by the lived material precarity that often structures life possibilities in the Global South for trans and travesti subjects.

Many of this special issue's contributions speak to uneven proximities to state violence and precarity by centering intimate exchanges among social agents, tactics of care, and resistance that defy state logics. As these articles make clear, multiple forms and practices of *compañerismx* generate unexpected solidarities and energize struggles against increased state austerity measures, heightened militarization, and expanded social and economic abandonment. Lohana Berkins's and Diana Sacayán's powerful travesti politics, grounded in material reparations and intersectional coalition, mobilize friendship as one such potent and sustained political response.

TSQ: Transgender Studies Quarterly ★ Volume 6, Number 2 ★ May 2019
DOI 10.1215/23289252-7348426 © 2019 Duke University Press

Figure 1. *Resistencia Trava.* Travesti activist Lohana Berkins at her last pride march demands justice for travesti activist Diana Sacayán, November 2015, Buenos Aires. Photograph by travesti activist Florencia Guimaraes García.

This special issue emerged from a series of four conference panels organized by a de la maza pérez tamayo, Claudia Sofía Garriga-López, Alba Pons Rabasa, and Cole Rizki for the conference Trans Studies*: An International, Transdisciplinary Conference on Gender, Embodiment, and Sexuality held at the University of Arizona in Tucson in September 2016. The panels brought over twenty scholars from the Global South and Global North into conversation across disciplines and methods. From the energy generated at that conference, Garriga-López and I proposed a special issue of *TSQ* and sought out senior scholars Juana María Rodríguez and Denilson Lopes to help bring this project to fruition. "Trans Studies en las Américas" received seventy-nine submissions written in English, Spanish, or Portuguese, a record number for the journal. Submissions arrived from countries across the hemisphere and addressed a broad range of topics in contemporary cultural production, public policy, education, and religion, through disciplines including anthropology, visual culture studies, literary criticism, performance studies, and sociology. The wide-ranging topical coverage, innovative methodological contributions, and geopolitical distribution of the seventy-nine submissions evince the pressing need for publication opportunities that feature Latin/x American and Caribbean studies scholarship—most especially by scholars situated in the Global South.

In this issue, we use the term *Latin/x America* to mark both Latinx and Latin American contributions and to insist on the entanglements of "US" and "Latin America" as geopolitical categories, underscoring their inherent instabilities. Indeed, many of our authors' institutional locations and geographic movements reflect such incoherence. Some of our authors are currently located in the United States yet were born or grew up in Latin America and are embedded within circular migration patterns or diasporic dispersals that further unsettle area and identity configurations. These complex, often unpredictable, and at times forced border crossings similarly trouble the fixity of geopolitical categories such as "Global North" and "Global South." Neither can be collapsed along topographic lines, and both should be understood as shifting and imbricated geopolitical formations that speak to the many circuits through which the majority of our authors move (or cannot). We simultaneously recognize the material and academic privilege that institutional location in the Global North affords even as our contributors' irreducible "translocations" call for nuanced readings of geopolitics and local class formations (Alvarez et al. 2014).

Throughout the editorial process, a number of issues symptomatic of trans studies' institutional precarity emerged. Academics situated in Latin America, for example, do not currently have access to trans studies faculty or research positions within university settings. Scholarship produced from the Global South on trans and travesti embodiment, subjectivity, cultural production, or activisms has largely been produced by nontrans academics from both the Global North and Global South—a condition that trans and intersex activists such as Mauro Cabral have vocally critiqued. In the north, trans studies positions are only recently starting to emerge. Rarely do these positions emphasize the Global South, and they remain vulnerable to institutional proclivities within an increasingly volatile neoliberal landscape. Scholars migrating to the north to access these increased opportunities are confronted with new challenges, including shifting racial hierarchies, anti-immigrant sentiment, and discrimination based on accent, and are obligated to produce scholarship in English. Academics across the hemisphere and elsewhere are impacted by the global demands of the academic market and its valuation of English-language publication.

Discrimination—both institutional and otherwise—has left many trans and non-binary-identified people outside of higher education and formal education more broadly, particularly in the Global South (Andrade 2012; Berkins 2005, 2015; Martínez and Vidal-Ortiz 2018). These conditions of discrimination and exclusion for trans, travesti, and non-binary-identified scholars, compounded by issues of race, immigration, and language, generate significant barriers to both institutional access and publication opportunities (see Cabral in Boellstorff et al. 2014: 423–24). The paucity of trans-identifying Latinx trans studies scholars and the overburdened conditions under which they labor create cumulative layered effects that impact submissions, the availability of peer reviewers, and our own editorial board composition. Our special issue, dominated by graduate students and junior faculty, thus underscores the tenacity of scholars working in a field that remains underresourced and undervalued throughout the hemisphere. Despite these challenges, "Trans Studies en las Américas" offers an exceptional and timely collection of Latin American and Latinx trans and travesti theoretical, (auto) ethnographic, political, and artistic production that speaks to the field's vibrancy.

Throughout *las Américas*, trans studies take multiple forms: scholarly work on identitarian and anti-identitarian analytics, interventions into state practices, aesthetic eruptions of creative energies, and strategic activist mobilizations. These modes of inquiry and critical approaches are regionally inflected by the flows of people, ideas, technologies, and resources that shape contemporary trans studies, opening space to explore the productive contradictions and expansive possibilities within this body of work. "Trans Studies en las Américas" highlights the analytic tensions that occur in highly localized sites. Such a move underscores the inherent problems with framing Latin America as a singular geopolitical formation, pointing instead to the ways in which embodied political practices unfold within geographic and temporal particularities. Once situated side by side, however, these articles work to curate critical conversations among trans studies scholars exploring how shifts in cultural epistemologies, aesthetics, geographies, and languages enliven regional theorizations of politics, subjectivity, and embodiment.

"Trans Studies en las Américas" brings existing Latin/x American subjectivities, activist strategies, and theories such as travesti into conversation with US-oriented trans studies to ask what sorts of political coalitions and embodied forms of resistance might be possible. While in English, *transgender* often needs to be modified in order to respond to local hierarchies of race, class, ability, and other forms of difference, *travesti* underscores instead the impossibility of such disarticulation in the first place. Nonetheless, *travesti* is not meant as a corrective to trans, and our authors do not expand the notion of trans to include *travesti*. Instead, many of the essays in this issue center *travesti* as an identification, a critical analytic, and an embodied mode of politics.

"Travesti," writes Malú Machuca Rose in their contribution to this issue, "is the refusal to be trans, the refusal to be woman, the refusal to be intelligible." Travesti theory and identification is a Latin/x American body of work and a body politics with an extensive transregional history (Campuzano 2008; Campuzano et al. 2013; Berkins 2003; Rodríguez 2015; Wayar 2018). The work of this issue's authors, including Machuca Rose, Dora Silva Santana, and Martín De Mauro

Rucovsky, demonstrates how travesti identification operates as a politics, a critical mode, and an epistemology. To quote Machuca Rose:

> Travesti is classed and raced: it means you do not present femininely all of the time because you cannot afford to. It means the use of body technologies to transform one's body does not come from a doctor's office but from resourcefulness in the face of *precarización*, the act by which the matrix of domination makes our bodies and our lives precarious. *¿Más clarito?* It means you get creative, you use your pens for eyeliner, get your hormones and silicones from your friends underground, or use *tinta* instead of *testosterona* to transform your body.

As a politics of refusal, travesti disavows coherence and is an always already racialized and classed geopolitical identification that gestures toward the inseparability of indigeneity, blackness, material precarity, sex work, HIV status, and uneven relationships to diverse state formations (Guimaraes García 2017). To claim travesti identity is to embrace a form of opacity and fugitivity that resists necropolitical systems that pointedly rely on capture (see Santana's contribution to this issue). Indeed, *travesti*, writes Santana, is "a negation of an imposed dominant expectation of womanhood that centers on people who are cisgender, heteronormative, able-bodied, elitist, and white." Travesti identification thus subverts both normative expectations of femininity and trans politics structured around assimilation and respectability. Claiming "travesti," as our authors make clear, is a way of inhabiting these complex histories of survival and resistance.

Travesti is certainly not a universal identification and some of the articles in this issue—those by Sayak Valencia and Cynthia Citlallin Delgado Huitrón, for example—do not engage the term. Neither is the term *travesti* equally distributed across the southern hemisphere; trans and travesti identifications are constantly shifting and should not be understood as mutually exclusive. The tensions between trans and travesti as identificatory categories are often untranslatable, leading us to ask what sorts of limitations and possibilities are embedded within the terms' distinctions and critical affinities. If trans men, for example, do not identify as travesti—at the time of writing, few would claim this term—what sorts of recourse do trans men have to localized identification if not *trans*? How can we account for the complex negotiations and appropriations that trans men enact in and through language in order to claim trans identification? The use of both *trans* and *travesti* throughout this introduction, and this special issue more broadly, is meant to underscore rather than settle these questions.

A turn to trans studies en las Américas further requires situated attention to experiences of state violence, including contemporary dictatorship and genocide, which necessitate theories that can account for the vulnerability of subjects and the urgency of public address. One way that existing trans studies scholarship has responded to such demands to theorize transnational experiences of state violence is through an expanded articulation of necropolitics. Achille Mbembe's foundational work "Necropolitics" (2003) complicates and reshapes Michel Foucault's articulation of biopower to theorize racialized zones of death. For Mbembe, biopower remains "insufficient to account for contemporary forms of subjugation of life to the power of death" (39). Necropower and necropolitics instead signal how power generates "forms of social existence in which vast populations are subjected to conditions of life conferring upon them the status of *living dead*" (39–40). Indeed, "politics," reminds Mbembe, is "the work of death" (16).

Engaging Mbembe's formulation of the necropolitical, C. Riley Snorton and Jin Haritaworn's foundational claims in "Trans Necropolitics: A Transnational Reflection on Violence, Death, and the Trans of Color Afterlife" (2013) offer vital critiques both for and of trans studies. These authors critically examine how activisms simultaneously devalue trans-of-color life while mobilizing trans-of-color death to vitalize homonormative and trans-normative activist projects, asking, "How do the biopolitics and necropolitics of trans death and trans vitality play out on the privileged stages of North America and Europe?" (67). Shifting the geopolitics of Snorton and Haritaworn's argument, this special issue moves the primary site of necropolitical inquiry from the United States and Europe to Latin America. In consequence, the circulation of travesti and trans deaths and, indeed, the very concept of an "afterlife" (66) hold alternate valence given shifts in state formation and contemporary experiences of genocide and dictatorship. In the context of truth commissions like CONADEP in Argentina and resulting publications like *Nunca más* or the Valech and Rettig reports in Chile that respond to genocide, logics of enumeration and descriptions of death and torture form an integral part in both these processes' and documents' reparative premises, claims to veracity, and epistemological authority even as these reports disregard experiences of trans and travesti death during dictatorship.[1]

In this vein, and making an important intervention into studies of state-sponsored terror, in their contribution to this issue Hillary Hiner and Juan Carlos Garrido describe ethnographic interviews they conducted with trans and travesti informants throughout Chile whose testimonies were excluded from official reports of state violence during dictatorship. Through oral histories, these trans and travesti subjects spoke of experiencing extreme forms of torture and mutilation. Even as we recognize the scholarly necessity of explicitly describing torture and violence as a corrective to archival erasure in dominant historical accounts, we remain cautious about the cumulative effects of discursively reproducing that harm. Several questions arose for us as editors: When is the scholarly reproduction of violence necessary, and when might that reproduction become another instantiation of harm? How might the answer to this question shift in relation to history, geopolitical location, readerly expectations, or subject position? And how are these issues complicated by the transnational circuits of exchange through which representations of violence are mediated? As work by our contributors suggests, the "archive of violence and anti-violence discourse" shifts radically across sites, necessitating sustained and increasingly nuanced discursive analyses that can account for divergent violence and antiviolence discourses in relation to shifting state and racial formations (Snorton and Haritaworn 2013: 67).

This issue further asks how trans death is mourned and remembered by travestis and trans women situated in the Global South. The articles by Valencia, Delgado Huitrón, and Hiner and Garrido all respond to this latter question, opening up important lines of inquiry that underscore social and political agency, as well as political practices that generate alternative forms of mourning and justice where none has been served. This special issue thus provides a supplement to existing necropolitical theorizations by focusing on trans agency and resistance in Latin/x America to technologies of value extraction and toxic political projects that feed off of trans death in the Global South to mobilize trans- and homo-normative activist and scholarly agendas.

In response to varying necropolitical conditions, many of the contributors to "Trans Studies en las Américas" explore embodied responses to state violence. These authors develop an ethics of care that teases out the "legacies of already everyday ongoing practices of caring for one another" to ask, "What do you do as a living being? What do you do to heal?" (Santana). Both Delgado Huitrón and Valencia take up this question in relation to the Mexican state. Delgado Huitrón's piece dialogues with the ongoing performance project *Proyecto 10Bis* by Mexican trans-feminist performance artist and activist Lia García (La Novia Sirena). Delgado Huitrón refigures the Spanish-language verb *trastocar*—to disrupt, upset, or perturb—as *transtocar*, literally "transtouch," to ask how Lia's hyper-tender, translative, and relational touch contests Mexican state hyperviolence. Delgado Huitrón turns to the haptic *as* tactic to explore how Lia's performance practice "enacts the potentiality of trans-, particularly as a labor of care: as a tender caress." In contrast, Valencia elaborates a "postmortem/transmortem politics" as a critical mode of bodily manifestation after death. Such an intervention politicizes the corpse by "using the presentation of the dead body to dignify it and avoid its erasure." As an example, Valencia's article centers an unlikely response to trans sex worker Paola Sánchez Romero's assassination. En route to the cemetery with Paola's body, her *compañeras* instead drive her coffin to the corner where she was assassinated, staging an impromptu open casket protest. Such a demand for justice inverts (trans)feminicide's dominant visual logics where the devastated, mutilated (trans) femme body is simultaneously spectacularized and banalized through mediatic reproduction. In a geopolitical context where, as Valencia writes, "every four hours a girl, a young or adult woman, is killed," postmortem/ transmortem politics responds to "Mexican social anesthesia around (trans)feminicide," denouncing Mexican state impunity.

Santana's article addresses the critique of necropolitics quite differently, focusing on dynamic forms of trans and travesti living and surviving. In the process, her work provides a compelling counterpoint to Valencia's, cautioning that, "despite the fact that it is fundamental to honor the dead by demanding justice, there is a risk that trans women, especially black trans women, are discussed only as a corpse" where "the deaths of trans and black people mobilize more action than our living, our *vivência*." Santana responds by elaborating *mais viva* (being more alive or more alert) as a form of "embodied knowledge" forged within "the imbrications between experiences of violence and the ways we find joy," to consider how travesti, transsexual, and trans women of color generate forms of everyday intimacy to resist death.

Shifting attention to the Southern Cone, Hiner and Garrido draw on oral histories and ethnographic interviews the authors conducted with trans, travesti, and transsexual women throughout Chile to examine how these subjects experienced Chilean state terrorism during Augusto Pinochet's dictatorship (1973–90). Mobilizing trans, travesti, and transsexual women's *testimonios*, the authors expand and reimagine what has remained a largely cissexist and heteronormative testimonial archive to include trans and travesti voices. Martín De Mauro Rucovsky's article similarly engages a pivotal moment in Southern Cone history, crafting a genealogy of Argentina's Ley de Identidad de Género (2012), or Gender Identity Law. De Mauro Rucovsky analyzes the trenchant travesti critique that the law reproduced binary logics by erasing the possibility of the legal category "T" for trans- and travesti-identifying subjects. Engaging in close readings of the law's articles, the author argues that the law is instead a social and political "strategic field of action" that suggests possibilities for radical, popular class political and activist alliances.

Machuca Rose's contribution engages in performative writing to explore transnational trans, nonbinary, and travesti identifications through storytelling, ancestry, and alternate kinship models. Through autoethnographic, performative writing, Machuca Rose writes alongside *ancestras*, or feminine ancestors, to explore "forms of interdependency and care among the living, the living-dead, and the dead." To do so, Machuca Rose engages with Giuseppe Campuzano's life, death, politics, and performance and installation piece *El Museo Travesti del Perú* (*The Travesti Museum of Peru*). Indeed, one of the most powerful interventions that Machuca Rose makes is to center HIV/AIDS infection, insisting on the centrality of sex and the politics of HIV to trans studies. Through performative trans feminist writing as creative and collaborative praxis, Machuca Rose cultivates a genealogy of ancestrality as "an impure family"—"*mi familia infecta*: the families we create out of our impure blood, our abject bodies, and undesirable fluids." Through this alternate form of abject kinship where fucking, touch, tenderness, and exchange operate as methodology, ancestrality results from connections forged "through a lifeline of blood and semen, infectious fluids carrying both danger and pleasure, creating our own deadly bloodlines." Machuca Rose ultimately suggests a politics of community rooted in radical interdependency, devotion, and care.

We have also included transcultural production throughout this special issue. The poem "Kiss" by Susy Shock, one of Latin America's best-known trans poets, is a carnal and tender response to abandonment and violence that echoes Lia García's performance practice and Delgado Huitrón's work on the caress. Artist Lino Arruda's cartoon provides a humorous take on transition and transmasculine embodiment—a topic notably absent from most of our seventy-nine submissions yet extremely urgent. Finally, the Trans Memory Archive project recuperated over six thousand photographs taken by trans women and travestis living across Argentina or in exile between the 1930s and early 2000s. A small selection of these powerful images is included here, as well as brief excerpts from interviews with the archive's creators; both images and text likewise serve as testaments to trans vitality.

"Trans Studies en las Américas" does not aim to be exhaustive or fully representative of Latin/x American trans studies. These articles represent a modest selection of the powerful work being done in the field, and this special issue portrays just one iteration among a multitude of forms that Latin/x American trans studies will undoubtedly take in the years to come. Neither does this special issue attempt to resolve the complex dynamics of representation raised by writing with and across forms of difference. While all of this special issue's authors and editors share elements of identification with the lives, research, and activisms represented in this issue, we all contend with the impossibility of fully accounting for alterity—whether our own or others'. Indeed, as this issue makes clear, such differences exceed geopolitical location and gender, extending to HIV status, engagement in sex work, immigration, and proximity to precarity and violence. What this collection of articles offers are models of collaboration and care among artists, activists, and academics committed to more just and livable futures.

Cole Rizki is a transgender studies scholar and a PhD candidate in the Program in Literature at Duke University. His research interests include hemispheric approaches to trans studies, Latin/x American studies, and visual culture and performance studies.

Acknowledgments

The special issue editors would like to acknowledge the LGBT Citizenship Cluster at the Haas Institute for a Fair and Inclusive Society at the University of California, Berkeley, for their financial support for this issue.

Note

1.   CONADEP or Argentina's National Commission on the Disappearance of Persons was a truth commission established in 1983 by then President Raúl Alfonsín to investigate the fate of thirty thousand disappeared citizens. The commission published the report *Nunca Más* (*Never Again*; 1984). For Chilean National Truth and Reconciliation Commission reports, see the *Rettig Report* (Comisión Nacional de Verdad y Reconciliación 1996) and the *Valech Report* (Comisión Nacional sobre Prisión Política y Tortura 2005).

References

Alvarez, Sonia E., Claudia de Lima Costa, Verónica Feliu, Rebecca J. Hester, Norma Klahn, and Millie Thayer, eds. 2014. *Translocalities/Translocalidades: Feminist Politics of Translation in the Latin/a Americas*. Durham, NC: Duke University Press.

Andrade, Luma Nogueira de. 2012. *Travestis nas escolas: Assujeitamento e resistência a ordem normativa*. Rio de Janeiro: Metanoia Press.

Berkins, Lohana. 2003. "Un itinerario político del travestismo." In *Sexualidades migrantes: Género y transgénero*, 127–37. Buenos Aires: Scarlett Press.

Berkins, Lohana. 2005. *La gesta del nombre propio: Informe sobre la situación de la comunidad travesti en la Argentina*. Buenos Aires: Ediciones Madres de Plaza de Mayo.

Berkins, Lohana, ed. 2015. *Cumbia, copeteo y lágrimas: Informe nacional sobre la situación de las travestis, transexuales y transgéneros*. 2nd ed. Buenos Aires: Ediciones Madres de Plaza de Mayo.

Boellstorff, Tom, Mauro Cabral, Micha Cárdenas, Trystan Cotten, Eric A. Stanley, Kalaniopua Young, and Aren Z. Aizura. 2014. "Decolonizing Transgender: A Roundtable Discussion." *TSQ* 1, no. 3: 419–39.

Campuzano, Giuseppe. 2008. *El Museo Travesti del Perú*. Peru: Institute of Development Studies.

Campuzano, Giuseppe, José Gabriel Chueca, Miguel A. López, Marcos R. Motta, and Centro Cultural de España (Lima). 2013. *"Saturday night thriller" y otros escritos: 1998–2013*. Lima: Estruendo Mudo.

Comisión Nacional de Verdad y Reconciliación. 1996. *Informe de la Comisión Nacional de Verdad y Reconciliación sobre Violación a los Derechos Humanos en Chile 1973–1990* [*Rettig Report*]. Santiago, Chile: Ministerio Secretaría General de Gobierno.

Comisión Nacional sobre Prisión Política y Tortura. 2005. *Informe de la Comisión Nacional de Prisión Política y Tortura* [*Valech Report*]. Santiago, Chile: Ministerio Secretaría General de Gobierno.

CONADEP (National Commission on the Disappearance of Persons). 1984. *Nunca Más: Informe de la Comisión Nacional sobre la Desaparición de Personas*. Buenos Aires: EUDEBA.

Guimaraes García, Florencia. 2017. *La Roy: Revolución de una trava*. Buenos Aires: Puntos Suspensivos Ediciones.

Martínez, Juliana, and Salvador Vidal-Ortiz, eds. 2018. *Travar el saber: Educación de personas trans y travestis en Argentina: Relatos en primera persona*. La Plata, Argentina: Universidad Nacional de La Plata.

Mbembe, Achille. 2003. "Necropolitics." *Public Culture* 15, no. 1: 11–40.

Rodríguez, Claudia. 2015. *Cuerpos para odiar*. Self-published *cartonera*.

Snorton, C. Riley, and Jin Haritaworn. 2013. "Trans Necropolitics: A Transnational Reflection on Violence, Death, and the Trans of Color Afterlife." In *The Transgender Studies Reader 2*, edited by Susan Stryker and Aren Z. Aizura, 66–77. New York: Routledge.

Wayar, Marlene. 2018. *Travesti: Una teoría lo suficientemente buena*. Buenos Aires: Muchas Nueces.

Trans Memory Archive

MARÍA BELÉN CORREA (founder), CECILIA ESTALLES,
CARLA PERICLES, IVANA BORDEI,
MAGALÍ MUÑÍZ, and CAROLINA FIGUEREDO

Together Argentine activists María Belén Correa and Claudia Pía Baudracco dreamed of creating El Archivo de la Memoria Trans or the Trans Memory Archive. After Claudia Pía's untimely death in 2012, María Belén moved forward with the project and began collecting photographs from other Argentine transwomen in digital space. Using a closed Facebook group, transwomen uploaded personal photographs and shared anecdotes that spanned decades, finding one another again. As the project swelled, a small team of transwomen and professional photographers formed to begin digitizing photographs, scanning them in high resolution to preserve trans memory.

The Trans Memory Archive collective presently includes founder María Belén Correa, Cecilia Saurí, Cecilia Estalles, Ivana Bordei, Magalí Muñíz, Carolina Figueredo, Carlos Ibarra, Carla Pericles, and Florencia Aletta. Sharing *mate* and *chisme*, the team meets every Wednesday to exchange photographs and memories, passing prints from hand to hand. They remember their loved ones and nemeses alike, and they record oral histories each time another transwoman arrives with new photographs to scan. Most recently, the archive was awarded first place out of all competing archives in Latin America for the Preservación y Acceso Documental Prize granted by major foundation Ibermemoria Sonora y Audiovisual in recognition of the collective's efforts around document access and preservation. The images that follow (figs. 1–6) were selected from the archive and are followed by excerpts from interviews sought for this special issue and conducted by archive member Cecilia Estalles with a number of transwomen who form part of the archive's team.

Carla Pericles

We never could have imagined the shape that this project is taking. Something that started from nothing is becoming a true archive.

TSQ: Transgender Studies Quarterly ★ Volume 6, Number 2 ★ May 2019
DOI 10.1215/23289252-7348440 © 2019 Duke University Press

As far as the photographs that make up the archive go, we have treasures, especially the black-and-white photos. I think of them as treasures because they contain our memory. They're the only thing that we have to reclaim our past, since so few of us survive.

I see very few remaining emotional links. So many friends are missing— that died in accidents, that the military killed or disappeared during the dictatorship. And those of us that are still here carry memories with us of what we went through.

When I see the photos, my entire life comes back to me, and I am moved at having survived all that. It moves me, but recounting what happened also makes me feel brave, since I am one of the few survivors of my generation.

I love being part of the project and learning more each day because it excites me to learn to do new things. Now, I look at photos that come into the archive and I say, "This photo could enter an exhibition or a contest." I can see the photo for the part that would interest everyone else, something that I didn't see before.

Ivana Bordei

I work on the research pieces: I have to go through old magazines, police reports. Sometimes I'll go through the newspaper archives at the national library, and I enjoy it. I was raised with these police reports in my head.

It is worth so much for us to show society what we went through and how we lived back then. Lots of the photos are of trans people cooped up in hotel

Figure 1. From the collection of Gina Vivanco, Archivo de la Memoria Trans

Figure 2. From the collection of Gina Vivanco, Archivo de la Memoria Trans

rooms. Very little social life could be lived outside, in plazas, in restaurants. It always strikes me. I was a teen in the 1980s and still a young person in the 1990s. And society found out about the things that we lived through back then only because we were constantly in police reports: "A dead *travesti* found murdered." And it's still hard to believe that society has been indifferent to that slaughter. So,

Figure 3. From the collection of Gina Vivanco, Archivo de la Memoria Trans

when we say that we're teaching something to society, it takes a bit for me to believe it because we're still sharing this society with the same people that reported me because they didn't like how I looked in restaurants or in a supermarket.

I think that years ago we lived with more companionship because repression made us all equally vulnerable. Then, the word *sisterhood* truly existed. For us it may be a new word, but we've always lived with this camaraderie. There

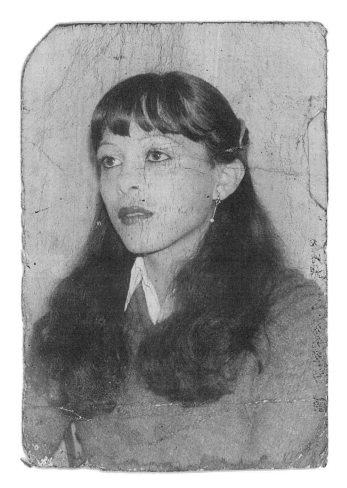

Figure 4. From the collection of Julieta González, Archivo de la Memoria Trans

have always been people that have helped out the younger ones. I don't know if *elder* is the right word because I remember that when I was a young girl the oldest woman I met must have been only thirty. They didn't have a chance at a long life. Nowadays, we're learning to get really familiar with old age as well.

Magalí Muñíz

The Trans Memory Archive is built from each of our experiences and with the life experience of the *compañeras* that donated and lent their photos for us to be able to have them and archive them. The photos are fantastic. Our very *compañeras* took them. Most of them are photos that we took at home because we didn't have the freedom to go out. And they're really valuable—they hold a lot of memories, a lot of feelings.

For me, what we make is art; it is a memory archive, but it is also art through the photographs, through the exhibitions, through everything that we're building.

Figure 5. From the collection of Claudia Pía Baudracco, Archivo de la Memoria Trans

I think photography has to speak for itself; the photos talk to you and tell you things. The difference between a photo taken by a photographer and one by us, I think, is the technique. We take casual photos. Technique is just as important as taking a photo with feeling, with care, with affection, with love for the person. Technique is important later so that the photo comes out well. The photos we've taken have more feeling. We take them in a nice, joyous moment, in a moment where we are happy, even if they're inside a house, but we were happy, celebrating a birthday, or having a drink, or smoking a joint, whatever. . . . For us, they were happy moments. They were photos taken with tenderness, with love.

Figure 6. From the collection of Claudia Pía Baudracco, Archivo de la Memoria Trans

Carolina Figueredo

The photographs excite me. I experienced it in the exhibition. The exhibitions were a total honor for me. I never thought that our photos were going to be seen by so many people. Truthfully, I felt proud for myself and my collective, that so many people started to see us. I saw myself in those histories. I went back thirty years, remembering, reliving those moments in my mind, seeing my *compañeras* from so many years ago with whom we shared moments together, good moments and bad. In the photographs, generally you see the few moments when we had the opportunity to get together. The exhibition helped me to relive the past. I never began to imagine that I was going to feel that, but it really moved me to see the photos.

Nowadays, the archive keeps us together. Now we meet up more. We chat more among ourselves. It's like we have a different space than what we had before.

From the moment we entered the archive, it was a spectacular experience for me. It was such an amazing idea—something that never really crossed my mind. I never pictured myself learning to digitalize a photo, to scan, to find value in a photograph. Maybe before I didn't see as much value in a photo as I do now. I'm learning to value something that I didn't even think about before.

Personally, it changed me so much, working in the archive, in my spirit; it raised my self-esteem because I began to get in touch with other people, to keep my mind busy, to clear up a lot of things that maybe I didn't even realize because I was coming out of a not-so-good time in my life, and this changed me a lot. For me it was an important step. If it hadn't been for the archive, our stories would never have been seen. Our photos never would have been exhibited. It's like the archive gave us the opportunity to scream out our pain at the top of our lungs, what we felt and what we lived.

When I began to scan photos, when I attended the exhibitions, I realized the value that these photos have because each photo represents a story. I hadn't understood that value before, and being in the archive helped me to understand.

I feel a little like a photographer because I enjoy it.

María Belén Correa is an internationally renowned trans activist from Argentina and the founder of the Trans Memory Archive. María Belén cofounded two of Argentina's first travesti and trans organizations including the Asociación Travestis, Transgéneros y Transexuales de Argentina (ATTTA) as well as REDLACTRANS, the Latin American and Caribbean Network of Transgender People. In 2004, she was granted political asylum in the United States, becoming the first Argentine trans person to be granted asylum outside Argentine after Argentina's democratic transition. She cocurated the exhibition *Esta se fue, a esta la mataron, esta murió* (2017) in the Haroldo Conti Cultural Center of Memory. She considers herself a survivor and now lives in Germany.

Cecilia Estalles is a thirty-six-year-old nontrans lesbian artivist from Buenos Aires whose artistic interests intersect with projects and collectives of social and political nature. She is interested in expanding the horizons and imaginaries of photography and in generating tools for social change. Since 2014, she has worked in the Trans Memory Archive, cocurated the exhibition *Esta se fue, a esta la mataron, esta murió* (2017), and deals primarily with the archive's administration.

Carla Pericles is a sixty-six-year-old trans woman from Tigre and the eldest member of the archive. She considers herself a survivor and spent twenty years living in exile in Italy. For the past year and a half, she has worked with the archive to digitize photos and co-curate exhibitions including *Esta se fue, a esta la mataron, esta murió* (2017). She is also in charge of administrating finances for the archive, which operates independently, with limited budget, and on a volunteer basis.

Ivana Bordei is a forty-six-year-old trans woman from Jujuy Province who has worked with the archive for the past two years. As part of her work with the archive, she spends time in the national library investigating archival photographs, magazines, newspapers, and police chronicles to piece together trans women's and travesti history. Ivana cocurated the exhibition *Esta se fue, a esta la mataron, esta murió* (2017), and she considers herself a survivor.

Magalí Muñíz is a fifty-four-year-old trans woman from Tigre who has worked in the archive for one and a half years. Her role with the archive consists of photo digitization, preservation, cataloguing, and conservation, and she also cocurates archival exhibitions, including *Esta se fue, a esta la mataron, esta murió* (2017). This year she has begun to study photography, and she considers herself a survivor.

Carolina Figueredo is a fifty-six-year-old transwoman from Neuquén Province who, as a trans elder, considers herself a survivor. Figueredo became affiliated with the Archivo de la Memoria Trans through Magalí Muñíz and has worked in the archive for the past one and a half years. As part of her work, she cleans and conditions photographs, preparing them to be digitized, and she cocurated the exhibition *Esta se fue, a esta la mataron, esta murió* (2017).

The Trans Memory Archive runs entirely by donation. While publication in an academic journal such as *TSQ* generates scholarly recognition for this activist project, it does not alter the material conditions of labor required to continue this work and can even serve as a form of extractivism. If you would like to make a donation to the archive to help ensure its longevity and directly impact the material conditions of this labor, please consider doing so at www .paypal.com/archivotrans.

Haptic Tactic

Hypertenderness for the [Mexican] State and the Performances of Lia García

CYNTHIA CITLALLIN DELGADO HUITRÓN

Abstract In 2017, Mexican transfeminist artist and activist Lia García (La Novia Sirena) made weekly visits to dorm 10Bis of the prison Reclusorio Norte, engaging in performative actions with a group of cis-male prisoners. Sprouting from images of *Proyecto 10Bis* (2017), this article argues that, within conditions of increasing violence and impunity, Lia transgenders touch in ways that, by (re)producing hypertenderness, serve as a balm for a hyperviolent state. Unpacking the haptics in the mechanics of production, and considering the Derridian impossibility of tact and of the law, the author argues that by placing herself—*cuerpo y corazón*—between the state and the body, Lia engenders a haptic tactic that, through a transgendered hypertender touch, activates transaffective resistances that contend with the law and the state.
Keywords performance, tenderness, touch, transgender, prison

> It is a problem [*aporia*] whether touch is a single sense or a group of senses. It is also a problem, what is the organ of touch; is it or is it not the flesh? . . . On the second view, flesh is 'the medium' [*to metaxu*] of touch, the real organ being situated farther inward.
> —Aristotle, *Peri psuches*

> Poner el corazón es, para mí, lo que subvierte esa línea entre la fisura y la caricia que se le puede hacer al estado también como una transgresión absoluta.
> —Lia García

Dressed in a light peach-colored dress, a crown of pink flowers outlining her head, a woman stands in intimate embrace—cheek to cheek—with a man dressed in beige. Across his T-shirt the text "armani exchange" spreads horizontally and repeatedly. His tattooed arms surround her, his hands clasped at the

TSQ: Transgender Studies Quarterly ★ Volume 6, Number 2 ★ May 2019
DOI 10.1215/23289252-7348454 © 2019 Duke University Press

back of her waist. Entwined, her arms—elbows folding within his embrace—reach toward his neck; her hands rest on his shoulders. They both look intently, and intensely, at the camera, with eyes that stare flirtingly and smiles that reveal the whiteness of their teeth. To the right, in the distance, hangs a clothesline with clean clothing.

At first glance, this image is almost banal in its ordinariness, for it reads as a memento photograph—a *quinceañera* party favor. The photograph (fig. 1) is compositionally predictable in its curatorial facade, in its embrace and its heternormative coming-of-age posture. A second glance—that is, a hermeneutical, slowed down glance—triggers suspicions: in the background barbed wire crowns the edge of a concrete wall, a watchtower stands tall on the far left side: a deviance from norms. Multiple questions arise, in each answer a germination of the next: Who are they? Where are they? How did they get there? Who took this picture? What for?

The image depicts Mexican transfeminist artist and activist Lia García (La Novia Sirena) in tight embrace with a prisoner of the Reclusorio Norte, a male prison in the northern part of Mexico City. Although my eyes fixate on this particular image, it is but one in a series of photographs in Lia's personal diary and field notes, which she tenderly shared with me in anticipation of our encounter. Repeating a similar compositional architecture, these images capture and document instances of *Proyecto 10Bis*, an artistic intervention and performative project or, to use her own words, *un encuentro afectivo* (an affective encounter). Lia

Figure 1. Lia in a quinceañera dress with Javier. *Proyecto 10Bis*, Mexico City, 2016. Photograph by Ian Derek Alexander Rivas.

characterizes most of her artistic and performance work as affective encounters, not only to highlight the spatiotemporal aspect of the work but also to bring attention to the multiple affective fields that she inhabits and ignites in her artistic practice. In her body of work, she engages with the (dis)placing of her trans-body in and through space, as well as in and through numerous tropes of femininity, including the bride, the *quinceañera*, and the mermaid.[1] These multiple figures serve perhaps a counterintuitive function, for it is through Lia's trans-embodiment of these feminine archetypes that she foregrounds the performativity of gender and sexuality through ritual while revealing the subtle tensions found in our own complicity within these fantasies, avowing not just the pain but the potential for pleasure that they hold. Lia's main interests lie in the processes of transformation that are engendered by undergoing personal processes of transition and trans-embodiment, but her explorations also expand the individualized corporeal and bodily transformations, turning them into larger processes of societal transformation: "To me, dressing as a bride is a political act that has to do with activating festivity, with igniting loving communication between people and, most important, with making my trans experience a possibility for collective transformation" (García 2013).

The image described is an instance of *Proyecto 10Bis*, a long-term intervention that began in 2016 when Lia started visiting the prison once a week to engage in conversations, workshops, and performative actions with a group of prisoners that live in dorm 10Bis of Reclusorio Norte, which gives name to this project. While the image is not the performance itself, it is my hermeneutical starting point. The image is important as a point of departure because it holds still for us that which cannot be contained: the multiple haptics—the touches—that piece together this affective encounter. Although the complexity of Lia's performative intervention expands through and beyond this image in its surface and its time, I use this image or, rather, its description both to mirror Lia and to ignite an initial "haptic visuality," a theory that Laura U. Marks and Dana Polan (2000: 22), in relation to film, describe as "a visuality that functions like the sense of touch." In this way, we enter—via a surface—the multidimensional space of the haptic by breaking down the illusion that understands sensorial knowledge as separable, breaking the containments of each sense. This article's main thesis approaches touch and the tactile in particular, but it takes as axiomatic that the haptic requires and, in fact, demands a disordering of the senses. Beyond the haptic as a properly constituted sense of touch, or the senses in general, it is helpful to think of the haptic as posited by Rizvana Bradley (2014: 1), as "the viscera that ruptures the apparent surface of any work, or the material surplus that remains the condition of possibility for performance."

The image described above is but one of the many surfaces of the performative project that is *Proyecto 10Bis*. The haptic in all its manifestations, that is, haptic visuality but, more precisely, tactility, is affective sensing beyond the surface. In this tactility lies a call to mix senses: to listen to images, to touch sounds, to smell proximity, "an inherited caress, its skin talk, tongue touch, breath speech, hand laugh. It is the feel that no individual can stand, and no state abide" (Moten and Harney 2013: 98). This multisensorial quality of hapticality is not synesthetic; rather, it is a relational way of sensing, a transitive action existing in a transitional moment of doing that ignites multiple senses. Thus, touch, at once a medium and an organ, is always already trans-: a sense that reaches beyond.

In the introduction to the *WSQ* special issue "Transgender," Susan Stryker, Paisley Currah, and Lisa Jean Moore (2008: 14) unpack the importance of the hyphen in *trans-* as one that opens up the space in between; if we understand *trans-* as the "capillary space of connection and circulation between the macro- and micro-political registers through which lives and bodies become enmeshed in the lives of nations, states, and capital-formations," then Lia's work inhabits, embodies, and acts precisely in that space, and with it the potential of trans-, through her material body, but also through her performative project *Proyecto 10Bis*. I develop the verb *transgender* alongside *touch* to bring attention to the embodiment of touch and the stickiness of its many affects. Standing at a stark contrast with the state and the law, in this article I argue that Lia transgenders touch in ways that serve as a balm for a hyperviolent state by (re)producing hypertenderness. To transgender touch means to activate it as a means and method—a haptic tactic that accesses affectivity to contend with the law and cope with state power.

Theorizing through and alongside Lia's hypertender touch reveals the materiality of the trans-ness of touch and its inherently migratory state: a constant movement, a dynamic state in between. To touch is to hail the other; hence, it is to involve the other in its doing. Thus, if touch is always already trans-, then to transgender touch—*transtocar*—may release its performative potential, particularly in relation to its ability to undo gender and sexuality as abided and prescribed by the law.[2] Furthermore, if this touch of trans-, by trans-, this transiting transgendered touch, is rendered hypertender, it stands at a stark contrast to the law, contending with the ontological limits it itself purports. This performatively engendered ontological limit causes an affective attachment to a social imaginary that the violence of the state would prescribe as deviant, illegal, threatening. To reveal transgendered touch as neither violent nor fearful; instead, rendering it hypertender serves as the antidote to the prescriptive hyperviolence of the law. Thus, a critique of violence is homologous to the analysis of the affective encounter that is *Proyecto 10Bis*, for if a hyperviolence defines the texture on which it unfolds, then hypertenderness exposes the bareness of life at the limits of death.

I begin the main part of this article with a brief contextualization of the space over which *Proyecto 10Bis* unfolds—an increasingly violent Mexico—in order to map a fractured topography not just touched by violence but largely constituted by it, as well as to begin locating Lia's fissuring touch. Then, taking the description of the image as a point of departure—as an opening—I use Tina Campt's theorizations of the haptic temporalities of images to foreground their mechanics of production, taking into consideration the ethical imperatives of production and circulation that frame images of violence. Having entered the haptics of this image, I expand the frame to address the haptics of the performance through an analysis of touch and tact, stemming from Jacques Derrida's deconstruction of their impossibility. Finally, in an aim to transgender touch and ungender tenderness, I unpack the form of the touch as it intersects with its embodiment—for Lia's trans- touch is decisively hypertender—to address what it means to use the haptic as method, as tactic, for trans-affective resistance.

Topographies of Violence/Fissures to the State

It is essential to address the context on which Lia's artistic interventions unfold, particularly *Proyecto 10Bis*, for it maps out the sociopolitical topography of the geographical region of Mexico and all the political, economic, and social significations that it as a sign bears. It is equally important to clarify that I put forth this contextualization not in an alarmist tone. Rather, I incorporate this element as a way to map out the specificities of the land and to expose how material violence becomes quotidian, becomes part of the conditions under which life, somehow, in spite of its impossibility—some life—continues to thrive.

The violence that configures the present conditions of Mexico is a complex web of interrelated mechanisms of power. Nowhere is this most convincingly illustrated than in philosopher and cultural critic Sayak Valencia's transfeminist conceptualization of "gore capitalism." In *Gore Capitalism* (2016), Valencia lucidly unpacks how the structures and dynamics of narcotrafficking have reconfigured all aspects—political, economic, social, cultural—of the spaces it inhabits and overtakes, claiming that Mexico, particularly its borderlands, is the epitome of such reconfiguration (Valencia 2011). The time and space of gore capitalism are one of necroempowerment, where the relationship of the narco with the state and with (neoliberal) capitalism is so intricately interwoven that their edges get blurred.[3] It is through necroempowerment, where the body itself is capital, and death has become the most profitable business, that we become a dystopia of globalization (Valencia 2016: 26). Such descriptions of and emphasis on violence are not a way to spectacularize it; rather, it is a manner to evidence what Valencia calls "side B" of globalization (25). Geopolitically located, gore capitalism manifests in ultraviolent practices that subalterns or marginalized subjects engage in to contend with the forces of the first world, that is, with globalization.

In a space constantly exposed to the touch of violence, it is no surprise that Mexico is fertile ground for further proliferation and aggravation of a stark gendered violence. This has led to the typification of the concept of feminicide, which allows for a visibilization and mapping of the power dynamics at the root of our gendered, raced, classed, and sexual relations, which further leads to a "shift [in] the analytic focus to how gender norms, inequities, and power relationships increase women's vulnerability to violence" (Fregoso and Bejarano 2010: 4). Furthermore, some of the material gains of this categorization are the construction of a legislative infrastructure with mechanisms that can be activated in key moments and the example of the (seldom) implemented Alerta de Género (Gender Alert) and the Ley General de Acceso de las Mujeres a una Vida Libre de Violencia (General Law of Women's Access to a Life Free of Violence). Because this violence does not act in isolation, the intersectional expansion of the concept as categorical mechanism becomes imperative. While the murder of transwomen is not a new phenomenon, their visibility in the media is increasing and, with it, initiatives to include them in the now established political and legal category of feminicides or as a category in and of itself, for which the term *transfeminicides* is being proposed and demanded (see, e.g., Radi and Sardá-Chandiramani 2016).

Although the existence of mechanisms of control for concepts deemed phenomena point toward an already broken system, the creation and expansion of legal categories intend to widen the legal structures that may permit legal action and overcome perceived impunity. The risks of living as women are real, material, and imminent. And although violence is not limited to these manifestations, what they reveal is the impossibility of locating their source, the messiness in which they exist, and the con-penetrability of fault. Similarly, adhering to the logic of the law and the state, justice, in the form of punishment, manifests in the shape of prisons, a mechanism intended to provide security, order, and, of course, justice—that impossible and unattainable desire. Prisons can therefore be understood as intersectional hubs where traces of gore capitalism are made evident.

To begin to unpack Lia's interventions, attention to the particularities of the penitentiary where *Proyecto 10Bis* transpires is crucial. The Reclusorio Norte, established in 1976 after the final closure of the Lecumberri prison, is a federal facility that houses three different types of inmates, indicted, processed, and sentenced, and where many prisoners await a trial for years, sometimes even a lifetime. The Reclusorio Norte has a number of basic resources and programs for the rehabilitation of its inhabitants. This seeming openness in the structure of the prison makes it a site for social workers and organizations, as well as creative and theater groups, to enter into the space with relative ease. In fact, it was in 2016, while working with Almas Cautivas, a nongovernmental organization dedicated to helping ensure that the rights of the LGBT communities in prisons are respected, that Lia's performative project sprouted. The Reclusorio Norte has an annex specifically destined for the LGBT community, presumably to safeguard their rights and provide a safe space for them within the prison. The micropolitics of this dorm, however, in its coexistence within the larger structure of the prison, often represent a higher incidence of violence for its trans- populations. Having experienced and witnessed the gendered spatial organization of the prison through activist work in the prison, Lia made a decision to engage in a different type of political work through performance and art, conceiving and executing *Proyecto 10Bis*.

Proyecto 10Bis was a long-term intervention that consisted of weekly visits to the Reclusorio Norte, where Lia engaged in organized conversation circles, workshops, and performative actions with a group of eight cis-male prisoners that live in dorm 10Bis. The intervention consisted of working sessions with a diversity of pedagogic and performative methodologies. Understanding her own body as an archive, Lia brought photographs, objects, and personal stories from the outside that were linked to her transition processes and that would elicit thoughts and conversations about family, love, and transition. In all sessions Lia paid close intimate attention to each of the men, engaging with them through sustained eye contact and through physical touch, often using "seduction as bridge for communication" (García 2017: 4).

While the Reclusorio Norte is not a high-security prison, not one that houses drug lords or high-profile offenders, in an all-encompassing gore capitalism it is not unreasonable to assert that the masculinities that dwell in such a space recall what Valencia terms *"endriago"* subjects, a monstrous subjectivity born out of a gore capitalism (Valencia 2016). For these rigid masculinities, the hegemony that governs the penitentiary, there is no space for trans- subjects or for transgendering acts. Lia's performance of everyday life is a disruption to gendered spaces, for despite embodying and performing femininity, the grain of her voice remains starkly masculine—a purposeful choice that denotes a commitment to her embodied politics. The inhabitants of 10Bis willfully chose to participate in Lia's intervention, very much in spite of the social sacrifices this entails for them, like undergoing *cabuleo*, a common term used within the Reclusorio Norte with a meaning akin to bullying (García 2017: 2). Importantly, the convicts that live in dorm 10Bis are men who have been deemed physically marked as a result of illicit activities. In Lia's words, "These bodies hold corporeal imprints such as gunshots, incomplete surgeries, or impacts of resistance linked to crime, positioning them as docile bodies in the eyes of the institution [of the state]" (García 2017: 1). Perhaps, Lia shared with me, this is what helped unite them initially. It is over and through the *machista*, heterosexual, and transphobic realities that Lia's touch intervenes, for in a space so starkly reigned by gender norms, Lia's performative project operates as a fissure through which her presence, her voice and her touch, destabilizes preconceptions of trans- embodiment.

The space of the prison, although the ultimate site of surveillance and control, is also governed by its own micropolitics and microeconomies. Thinking with Michel Foucault (1975: 3), the Reclusorio Norte functions not only like a panopticon but also like a heterotopia, a *real* space (as opposed to a utopia) that works as a countersite, where "real sites that can be found within the culture, are simultaneously represented, contested, and inverted." Their own social structures and economies do not just mimic what is outside their confinement but are branches of the hegemony that reigns it. By this logic, the gendered economies, through (or perhaps in spite of) the gender segregation of the prison, remain hegemonic normative gendered dynamics of domination, or machismo.

These micropolitics and quotidian prison dynamics, of course, affect the way in which nonprisoners enter, exit, and behave in such confined heterotopic spaces. The borders that delimit the prison are material manifestations of the limits that are drawn and redrawn by the law. When and where do we touch on these limits? How can we make fissures on the law—fracture those barbed wire walls—to transgress such borders? What enters and what escapes as we simultaneously caress and fissure to transgress?

Haptic Traces and the Mechanics of Production

The macropolitics and heterotopic micropolitics of the prison choreograph the way in which Lia—a "free" trans- woman—enters such a space, and even more so when she embodies and effects hypertender touch as method. To follow Lia's tracks as she leaves traces of her touch and to enter the space of the prison with her, I return to the photograph in question: barbed wire atop thick cement walls, a watchtower. This photograph is part of a documentation of a performative action that took place in February 2017 and is a new iteration of a previous piece Lia had performed in 2014 titled *Mis XXy años*. In that performance, Lia, dressed in a *quinceañera* dress, celebrates was she calls her "coming of gender" in a metro station in Mexico City to mark a specific time in her transition. For the iteration of the performance as part of *Proyecto 10Bis*, Lia entered the prison wearing a light peach pink *quinceañera* dress to celebrate her coming of gender with the male prisoners of dorm 10Bis. Entering the prison in a *quinceañera* dress marks a liminal entry point, for at every security filter Lia was stopped and asked questions. Voices asking *¿Dónde es la fiesta? ¿Puedo ser tu chambelán?* (Where's the party? Can I be your *quinceañera* date?) surrounded her, and she took each opportunity to engage facetiously and flirtingly with the curiosity of the guards and the people present (García 2017: 5). Once she arrived in dorm 10Bis, having

been enthusiastically escorted by other inmates excited to partake in this celebratory event, she settled with the men of 10Bis. With them, she spoke of the
archetype of the *quinceañera* and what it means for her in relation to her transition, much beyond its superficial popular connotations or its radical social
construct, engaging with the political tensions it creates. She talked to them
individually—in secret, whispering in their ears, what it was like for her to be a
trans- woman in Mexico, telling them about gendered violence, transitioning,
feminicide rates, and other things. Then, on the floor Lia drew a map, and one by
one she led them by the hand, or the waist, or the shoulder, allowing each one to
choose the form of the hold and the touch as they danced or walked across the
path. All throughout, a camera was present, simultaneously documenting the
work and partaking in the celebratory ritual.

Specifying artistic documentation as the reason for these images inclines
us to locate it in the genre of artistic archival photography, of documentation. The
subjects in the images, however, are men convicted of crimes who purposely
pose before a camera. In this photograph, taken in captivity, a hybrid genre is
engendered: at once a celebratory *quinceaños* memento and convict photo, an
artistic documentation and an image of war of sorts; a freezing of time as joyous
occasion, like a regular *quinceañera* portrait—the man reads as just one more of
Lia's *chambelanes*. At its surface, it evokes a desire to seize a moment of cele-
bration, perhaps of pleasure, through a purposeful posing; a desire to hold or
contain, through an ordinary pose, a moment of life, in spite of violence, where
death lies both outside and inside the frame. Consonant to Nicole R. Fleetwood's
(2015: 492) analysis of vernacular prison photography, these photographs display
the ambivalence of negotiating desires, representing "subjects of value against the
carceral state that defines them as otherwise." These photographs, then, are objects
caught somewhere between life and death, as reminder, and remainder, of both,
in spite of the other: a memento vivere and a memento mori at the same time.

To follow the haptic traces of this photograph and performance, I turn to
Campt's method in *Listening to Images* (2017) and her sensory approach to
photographs, particularly to what she terms haptic temporalities. For Campt,
haptic temporalities "include, but are in no way limited to, the moment of capture; the temporality of the photographic re/production of material objects; their
assembly and reconfiguration as nodes of state, social and cultural formation"
(72). To illustrate this, she turns to an archive of convict images in a photo album.
I pause in this particularity for, similarly, a problem of genre immediately reveals
itself. In the case of the convict photo album that Campt analyzes, one of their
final ends was to be part of a ledger, an album used for accounting. While Campt's
convict photos are not meant as photographs that circulate for a larger mediatized
audience, their purpose takes another, albeit different violent and colonial shape,

that of surveillance. Thus, the relationship between the photographic capture of each convict photo with the forms of state, carceral, and colonial accounting are made evident.

A photograph is simultaneously an image and an object. Tracing the haptic temporalities of a photograph is an approach that sprouts from touch itself and all its affective frequencies and horripilations. This act unpacks and breaks down the teleology of time through the various encounters that take place prior, simultaneous, or analogous to the existence of the photograph itself as object. It is a sensorial method that indexes the multiplicity of elements present in a frag- mented mechanics of production:[4] all the actions, interactions, movements, permissions, acts of witnessing, and assumptions necessary for (prior to) the actual production of the photograph, which, at the same time reveal, in part, its conditions of possibility. Foregrounding these conditions or mechanics of pro- duction is relevant for two reasons. First, it leads us to question what performative negotiations were made in order to reorder the conditions of possibility that allow for the performance of this action and, second, because leaving the analysis at the level of the surface of the performance does not address the full extent of its haptic dimension. In fact, attention to the mechanics of production may be an attempt to reach into the depth and span of the haptic, in search of the limits we touched (or didn't touch, or avoided) in order to touch the object, or image, we have before us, and for it to touch us.

Unpacking the mechanics of production of the photograph in question, we encounter, to continue following the thought of Campt, an initial haptic temporality in the moment of capture of a convict photo. However, the first haptic temporality of this convict/memento hybrid—this memento vivere-cum- mori—lies in a prior instance, for its touch with the law lies not at the moment in which the convict is forced to pose for and captured for years to come, as in Campt's convict photos. The limit of the law is touched even in the act prior to photographic capture, at the moment when Lia's body and the objects she bears enter the prison, crossing a border and hence touching the limits. This haptic temporality—one prior to the moment of capture—can be traced through the journey of two objects that allow for the existence of the photos: the camera and the dress.

The act of bringing these two objects into the prison is a condition nec- essary for the existence of these photographs and of the performance itself. How did these forbidden objects cross these seemingly intractable lines? Were they smuggled into the space, or were they casually permitted to enter? This act reveals the mechanics of production of both the photograph and the performance (both affective encounters in and of themselves). These objects, be they prosthetic elements of the performer or performers in and of themselves, cross a line; they break a rule. In this performance this line is quite literal, as it is marked passing the security gate, undergoing searches, and showing documentation of granted permissions to enter and exit the prison. In crossing this line, in breaking this rule, these objects denounce the imaginary aspect of the delimitations of such a space and the permeability of their materiality. In this penetrative choreography, in the act of crossing the lines, a series of resignifications, both of the objects themselves and of the lines that they cross, alters the temporal and material economies that structure life in prison. Furthermore, the material line of the security entrance to the prison is segregated by gender. As part of the intervention, Lia chooses to enter the prison from the man/male (hombres) entrance, despite, as she highlights, having all her "papers up to date." This seemingly small detail is one that hyperbolizes—exorbitantly—the deviance of her body. And yet Lia insists that her "body in transition," her abject body, one continuously grazed by violence, one disallowed as a body of or for desire, sensuality, and affect, be the space where this intervention in the penitentiary occurs.

In this line crossing, in this trans-gression, what these objects—these performances—do is touch the limit of the law, revealing its impossibility. They, to use Derrida's words in *On Touching—Jean-Luc Nancy* (2005), "touch without touching" the limit of the law, revealing not only the impossibility of law but also the impossibility of tact itself, for "tact, one could say, is what *confines* to the origin and the essence of law. And one should understand tact, not [only] in the common sense of the tactile, but in the sense of knowing how to touch *without* touching, without touching *too much*, where touching is already too much. Tact touches on the origin of the law. Just barely. At the limit" (67). In this Derridian understanding of tact, we must understand the multiple meaning of tact as both attached to the sense of touch—of the tactile—and as it adheres to laws of sociality, following or not following convention, tact as unspoken pact. Inextricable, as well, are the aforementioned haptics experienced through the mechanics of production of the/a performance, for the unpacking of touch itself is not understood, then, solely as sensory mode but simultaneously as method. Touch as method foregrounds its relationality, for, as it is not unidirectional, it depends on its surround—on its reactions—to shape what proceeds. Touch is a haptic tactic that opens up a space of possibility as it fractures and fissures the law.

Transgendering Touch/Ungendering Tenderness

Touch is always relational. There is directionality to touch, a transitiveness of touch, for there is a subject that exercises the action of touch and an object, on what or whom the action is exercised: that which is touched. Furthermore, it is not only who or what we touch but also who/what touches whom (with its own gendered laws), and how we touch whom/what we touch, and what that "how" does. Although Derrida warns us against jumping hastily to such subject/object relations, whom this touch is coming from is crucial here, because it speaks to how the embodiment of transgender can be thought of as a way of understanding, as a method of doing. Furthermore, tact and touch, in their impossibility, have a form (perhaps even their own tact).

Lia's touch is a caress. Although Derrida seemingly opposes two forms of touch, the blow (striking) or the caress (stroking), we can understand the caress as a stroke that, in its equivocation, strikes. In a world reigned by a touch that strikes, what may be engendered by a touch that strokes? Through this caress the law itself is reordered. Furthermore, Lia's caress is tender, and what this tenderness is doing is calling on the Other, beyond the "face," that is, encounter, intersubjectivity, and affect, beyond visuality. The sensing of the other through the touch of a caress, simultaneously—and not—a caress leads to what Derrida (2005: 81), in a riff off Emmanuel Lévinas, calls the "equivocation of the caress," where "in the untouchable's touching, the inviolable's violation, the caress threatens the ethical, since it carries beyond the face." But what goes "beyond the face," always following the same "contradiction" of "formal logic," is still a face, a "face that goes beyond faces." In taking up Levinas's exploration of the (voluptuous) caress, of the tender touch, Derrida falls into the abyss of the seemingly unavoidable: gendering this form of touch, an outdated adherence of tender to the feminine. The equivocation of the caress, its ambiguity-cum-ambivalence and its breaking of tact, Derrida (2005: 81) says, "is decidedly seen making an inscription on the side of the feminine, seemingly modifying, then verily defeating, in intentionality." This adherence is premised, of course, in heterosexuality.

Touch is always already charged with the erotic, with the sensual, not just the sensory, for touch engages in intersubjective desires: one cannot be without the other, for to touch is to hail the other, to face them. But Lia's touch is not just a tender caress; it is hyperbolic, excessive, *desbordada*. Lia's excessive touch and movement—"mi manera desbordada de moverme en la carcel" (García 2017: 2)—her overflowing and/or borderless manner of moving, this excessive form, hypertenderness, is enabled by gesture and executed through touch. It is a twofold transgression: by touching the material boundaries alive in the laws that govern the context of the prison, and by touching the material boundaries active in the laws that govern gender and sexuality. To transgender touch, then, means to transgress the lines and borders that delineate gendered expectations in the social imaginary, and the fantasy of its overdetermination. And thus, what the hypertender touch of Lia does is reorient desire and erotics, shifting the stickiness of body to gender to sexuality, and vice versa—while simultaneously ungendering tenderness by disrupting monolithic embodied understandings of both tenderness and femininity, leaving as residue its core form: care.

Hypertenderness, when (dis)placed within a context that represents hyperviolence—that cages those within its walls, in a space that represents the failure of containment, a place that represents the state's hand—becomes a balm. To hypertenderly touch hyperviolence is to tend to it. The touch that Lia exercises, or exerts, or exudes, from her own deviant (that diverges, diverts) and dissident (that differs, disagrees) embodiment—from her flesh—is one exerted through proximity, but also through the tactile: the hand that reaches out to tenderly touch. The hand as the means of touch, the mechanism through which purposeful touch happens, matters. Approaching this performance in relation to the tactile, particularly Lia's touch, Jeanne Vaccaro's (2015: 275) notion of the handmade becomes helpful, for "the performative dimensions of craft privilege the politics of the hand, that which is worked on, and the sensory feelings and textures of crafting transgender identity." If crafting transgender identity is a performative continuous action, we can never dissociate the craft from the hand and the hand from the touch and the touch from the tending. Vaccaro, like Lia, understands trans- not as an action but as an encounter, precisely that affective encounter that may lead to the "equivocation of the caress"—that ambivalent space of potentiality and possibility, namely of world making.

The handmade, Vaccaro (2015: 275) explains, privileges the labor of touch, and texture, to unsettle static understandings of transgender identity and direct it toward transgender as a practice of crafting, a craft made through touch and the hand, a particularly haptic practice: "By speaking of 'crafting' transgender identity, I mean to highlight the felt labor and traces of making and unmaking identity and the performative doing of gender becoming in relation to the materiality of the flesh." And so, the handmade posits the hand as that which makes, that which crafts, questioning what it means to craft identity. Lia's work, through her hand and her touch, expands this notion by crafting—through touch—a balm for the state.

Between the Fissure and the Caress

Lia's hand, reaching up and back over her left shoulder, gently touches the hand of a prisoner; her fingers just touch the surface of his skin. A pink sequin dress, long wavy brown hair crowned by coral flowers, long nude nails on her fingers, Lia uses her hand to lead him softly. His hand, arm extending over toward her shoulder, protected within the hold of Lia's hand, rests timidly yet assuredly on the bare skin of her shoulder. He follows her trustingly, his face tilted downward, his smiling eyes closed, revealing complicity, a quiet transgression. This haptic tactic is the caress and the fissure undistinguished.

And in the surround—still—the walls that enclose the building edged by a large spiral of barbed wire remind us of the space that extends beyond, of the limits of law and the scope of the performance. This performative moment, captured by a camera, becomes an image. If the mechanics of production of the photograph are the conditions of possibility for its existence, then the photograph's mere existence, like trans- embodiment itself—like the trans- body—depends on crossing, on transgressing boundaries, on touching the limits delineated by the law and the state. Lia's archive, in addition to or in spite of its trans-content, is a trans- archive itself in form. If not a trans- archive, definitely a transing archive: always in transition, active, fractured, and fracturing—never whole.

Lia embodies and inhabits that space of potentiality through the transgressive touch of her material body and the affective resonances of its form. The performative work of *Proyecto 10Bis* lies in that opening space—that aperture—that trans- as processual prefix engenders. Lia positions her body precisely in that between. Yet it is not just the presence of her dissident body, but what this body provokes. This performance, then, and all of the microperformances, the fissures, the disruptions, arouses and enacts the potentiality of trans-, particularly as a labor of care: as a tender caress. Lia's body and flesh are one that touches, a touching body. In this way Lia's tenderness touches the point between the law and the flesh. The relationship between state violence and trans- allows us to see what it means to transgender touch qua tenderness. If we understand the "touch of the law" as a striking, then transgendering touch may render it a stroking.

By exploring the haptic temporalities that stem from an image taken to archive the performance *Proyecto 10Bis*, we unveil the limits that are touched, and not touched, in the mechanics of production of an artistic intervention that seeks to transgress the boundaries of violence, the state and the law itself. Hypertenderness as balm—at the site/sight of the state, is a haptic tactic of potentiality in trans-gression. Transgendering touch and ungendering tenderness, *poner el corazón*, in the words of Lia, is precisely what "subverts that line between the fissure and the caress that can be done onto the state . . . as an absolute transgression" (García 2017: 1). The embodiment of Lia's touch, in an effort to expand the skin (*extender la piel*)—a surface—ignites affective resistance that transgress, that transgender, and that reorient desire and erotics. The tactile process of hypertenderness, then, may enable utopic longings as we touch on the possibilities of creating, or inhabiting, other worlds.

Cynthia Citlallin Delgado Huitrón is a PhD candidate in performance studies at New York University and an interdisciplinary artist from Mexico City. Her political, scholarly, and artistic interests lie at the intersection of aesthetics, politics, queer, and transfeminist performance and decolonial studies. She is currently serving as book reviews editor in the collective *Women and Performance: A Journal of Feminist Theory*.

Notes

1. Lia's engagement with these tropes has been a sustained practice that repeats in multiple performances. Some examples of each are *Mis XXy años* (2014) and *A la distancia* (2015). By engaging with these tropes and placing her own trans- body in relation to, or alongside, such rituals, Lia accesses the gendered and sexualized fantasies that they entail, revealing a dissonance between the material (body/flesh) and the discursive (archetypes), inhabiting the "in between"—a state of constant transition.

2. Theorizing across borders means engaging in constant processes of translation. For this reason, "to transgender touch" is conceived alongside a Spanish modification of the word *trastocar*. In the dictionary of the Real Academia Española, the verb *trastocar* is defined as (1) *trastornar o alterar algo*, (2) *trastornarse o perturbarse*, that is, (1) to disrupt, upset, or alter something, (2) to be disrupted or upset oneself, to be perturbed or perturb oneself. Adding the *n* in the middle of the word follows the understanding that "the prefix *trans* makes reference to something that traverses what it names, it re-vertebrates it and transmutes it" (Valencia 2016: 191). Therefore, *transtocar* (literally "transtouch"), I propose, does the work of incorporating the transgendering of touch, as it alters or "perturbs" semantically its relation to both gender and touch.

3. That is, "processes that transform contexts and/or situations of vulnerability and/or subalternity in the possibility for action and empowerment . . . reconfigured from within dystopic practices where perverse self-affirmation is achieved by way of violent practices" (Valencia 2016: 31n1).

4. I am thinking here with Denise Ferreira da Silva in *Toward a Global Idea of Race* (2007) and her notion that foregrounding "modes of production" may displace post-Enlightenment assumptions. However, I choose to use the phrase *mechanics of production* to highlight a more quotidian almost mechanical action in artistic production processes.

References

Bradley, Rizvana. 2014. "Introduction: Other Sensualities." *Women and Performance* 24, nos. 2–3: 129–33.

Campt, Tina. 2017. *Listening to Images*. Durham. NC: Duke University Press.

Derrida, Jacques. 2005. *On Touching—Jean-Luc Nancy*. Translated by Christine Irizarry. Stanford, CA: Stanford University Press.

Ferreira da Silva, Denise. 2007. *Toward a Global Idea of Race*. Minneapolis: University of Minnesota Press.

Fleetwood, Nicole R. 2015. "Posing in Prison: Family Photographs, Emotional Labor, and Carceral Intimacy." *Public Culture* 27, no. 3: 487–511.

Foucault, Michel. 1975. "Of Other Spaces: Utopias and Heterotopias." In *Diacritics* 16, no. 1: 22–27.

Fregoso, Rosa-Linda, and Cynthia Bejarano. 2010. "Introduction: A Cartography of Feminicides in the Américas." In *Terrorizing Women: Feminicide in the Américas*, edited by Rosa-Linda Fregoso and Cynthia Bejarano, 1–44. Durham, NC: Duke University Press.

García, Lia. 2013. "Diarios de una novia en acción: Más allá del beso se dislocan los sentidos." *Hysteria Revista*, no. 2. hysteria.mx/diarios-de-una-novia-en-accion-mas-alla-del-beso-dislocar-los-sentidos/.

García, Lia. 2017. "Extender la piel: Sobre el trabajo afectivo extendiendo el corazón." Dossier from personal diary entries, García's personal archive.

Marks, Laura U., and Dana Polan. 2000. *The Skin of the Film: Intercultural Cinema, Embodiment, and the Senses.* Durham, NC: Duke University Press.

Moten, Fred, and Stefano Harney. 2013. *The Undercommons: Fugitive Planning and Black Study.* Brooklyn, NY: Minor Compositions.

Vaccaro, Jeanne. 2015. "Feelings and Fractals: Woolly Ecologies of Transgender Matter." *GLQ* 21, nos. 2–3: 273–93.

Valencia, Sayak. 2011. "Capitalismo gore: Narcomáquina y performance de género." *E-misférica* 8, no. 2. hemisphericinstitute.org/hemi/en/e-misferica-82/triana.

Valencia, Sayak. 2016. *Capitalismo gore: Control económico, violencia y narcopoder.* Mexico City: Paidós.

Radi, Blas, and Alejandra Sardá-Chandiramani. 2016. "Travesticide/Transfemicide: Coordinates to Think Crimes against Travestis and Transwomen in Argentina." www.aacademica.org /blas.radi/15.

Stryker, Susan, Paisley Currah, and Lisa Jean Moore. 2008. "Introduction: Trans-, Trans, or Transgender?" *WSQ* 36, nos. 3–4: 11–22.

Necropolitics, Postmortem/ Transmortem Politics, and Transfeminisms in the Sexual Economies of Death

SAYAK VALENCIA

Translated by OLGA ARNAIZ ZHURAVLEVA

Abstract This article proposes two specific interventions, utilizing a critical transfeminist positioning to critique a transexclusionary perspective in writing and research on the crucial problem of
necropolitics and the murder of women in Mexican society: (1) the term *postmortem/transmortem
politics*, to reflect on the forms that imagination and political practice developed inside a Mexican
trans community to deal with the necropolitics that murders trans and cis women on an everyday
basis with complete impunity—in this sense, the process of mobilization, here called *postmortem/
transmortem*, builds bridges of transfeminist alliance since it reactivates and embodies struggles
against femicide and transfemicide from communities of care and vulnerability; and (2) the goals of
the transfeminist movement as a source of feminist repolitization and greater inclusivity for the
subject of feminisms, considering those subjects left outside or energetically moved away from the
neoliberal reconversion of the critical devices of the white heterosexual and institutional feminisms
that we know today as gender politics or "women's politics," managed and operated by the state.
Keywords transfeminisms, necropolitics, transpolitics, postmortem politics

This is a reflexive text that inserts itself in a larger research project about necropolitics and its production of violence against minoritarian becomings.[1] The basis of its methodology is participatory action research. This article argues for the need to build strategies and alliances in the extremely bloody context that sieges cis, trans, and nonbinary women in Mexico.[2] From a critical position against the trans-excluding and transphobic perspective, the text is written by a Mexicanx *fronteriza cuir* cis-gender woman, who participates actively both in academia and in transnational transfeminist activisms.[3]

TSQ: Transgender Studies Quarterly ★ Volume 6, Number 2 ★ May 2019 **180**
DOI 10.1215/23289252-7348468 © 2019 Duke University Press

The focus of this proposal draws from the transfeminist perspective, understood as the incorporation of transgender discourse into feminism that becomes an epistemic tool: "Transfeminism encompasses much more than the inclusion of trans people in feminist politics or their depathologization in the field of psychiatry. It is an epistemology—a theory of knowledge and power—that guides a diverse array of transfeminist activist political practices" (Garriga-López 2019: 1621). In this sense, transfeminisms are articulated as nonidentitarian networks of care and transnational dialogue, where the historic memory of the minoritarian becomings intersects with strategies of resistance and social transformation to build communities of emotional support and survival in a necroliberal context. To exemplify this, I present two interventions:

1. I propose the neologism *postmortem/transmortem politics* to think about the imagination and political practices that take shape inside a Mexican trans community that decides to protest publicly with the body of a murdered trans friend present among them, to confront the necropolitics that murders trans and cis women every day, with impunity, and that excludes them from the possibility of being read in a socially dignified way even after their death. In this sense, the process of mobilization that I here call postmortem/transmortem creates bridges of transfeminist alliance while at the same time reviving the struggles against femicide in communities highly exposed to social and state necropolitics.

2. I propose we use the goals of the transfeminist movement as a bridge for feminist repolitization and expansion of the subject of feminisms, considering the subjects left outside of or that strongly move away from the neoliberal reconversion of the critical devices of the feminisms that we now know as gender politics or that are reduced to "politics of women" to perform a token function (Kanter 1977) of these struggles against the neoliberal state.

Transfeminisms and Strategic Alliances as a Response to Gender-Based Violence and Necropolitical Masculinity

I say the word *death* and I shiver; I shiver in a country full of dead and disappeared people.[4] I say the word *death*, and then the word *feminisms* appears as one of the strongholds that still makes sense to think about life and sustainability politics against this binary, heteropatriarchal, and necro-neoliberal *cis-tem*.[5] However, saying the word *feminisms* is not an easy act, since it means talking about multiple currents, historical perspectives, situated strategies, locations, embodied experiences, and world views, on a political and personal level, that cannot be grasped or standardized to a definite version. Maybe in this difficulty to be standardized resides the key to the survival of the feminist movements; their having not just a name but multiple surnames activates their strategies and turns them into a highly networked movement full of processes and strategically situated actions.

To date, in Mexico, every four hours a girl, a young or adult woman, is killed. Women are being killed gruesomely, with extreme violence. Some of the causes of death described in the media and international reports are "mutilation, asphyxia, drowning, hanging, or with their throats slashed, burnt, stabbed or with gun wounds" (Muedano 2017). Women are killed, raped, displayed, and erased from the world with rage, with hatred from the patriarchy and the fraternities, with social ambush and judicial advantage.

Trans and gender-variant women are not only killed as women, with overflowing sexual brutality, but also killed socially for disobeying the biologist mandate of conforming to live in a body whose gender has been assigned medically and with which they do not identify. They are erased from the conceptual map of the possible and what can be enunciated. So far this year, the Trans Murder Monitoring Project has reported "325 cases of reported killings of trans and gender-diverse people" (Proyecto Transrespeto versus Transfobia en el Mundo 2017).

I started this section about transfeminisms with this reminder of numbers and deaths to talk about the state of emergency and the necropolitical and necroadministrative context in which trans women, cis-gender women, and other minoritarian becomings have to survive. I remember death because, unfortunately, it seems to be the common thread among dissident people, and because it is around this radical act that other ways of claiming visibility and justice are manifested.

It is important to reflect once again about systematic murder as the persistent center of the organization and spread of Western modernity-coloniality, because the expansive necropolitics displayed in our ex-colonial territories is not an exception to the biopolitical contexts where the life of the population is managed without expressive violence but a continuum of neocolonial governance, where death is a kind of civilizing technology that persists until today and connects the current context with colonial intermittency through the technologies of murder as a way of indoctrination. Thus, death is a driver of surplus for necropolitics and continuous plunder in our territories and people, which also activates sexual economies whose surplus is generated through the suppression of certain people produced as disposable or unwanted, radically denying them their "right to appear" (Butler 2015).

Thus, violence and death are common elements of the coloniality of gender (Lugones 2008), whose extreme consequence and ultimate aim are precisely the elimination of indigenous populations that have nevertheless endured settler colonialism (Kauanui 2016) and its five-hundred-year-long massacre against them. As Patrick Wolfe (1999) notes in his work on settler colonialism, populations that have been ravaged for being potentially unruly, populations whose intersections dismantle sexual dimorphism and denaturalize their oppression, also contradict the ideological architectures that construct the project of plunder, dominion, and exploitation of the modern West.

In the current context, it is urgent to make alliances among the feminist movements, since we are in a period where political mobilizations seem to make sense only in a postmortem way, where the main feminist slogans in circulation in Latin America and the Caribbean center around the demand to not be killed, as evidenced by the transnational movements represented on social media with the hashtags #NiUnaMenos and #VivasNosQueremos, and where the tools and discourses of our struggles are expropriated by fascist-like democracies through the cosmetic commodification of our political demands. In this social space of convergence between markets and protests, necropolitics expands as the "constitutive outside" (Butler 1993: 197) that fences us and wants us lifeless and segregated.

Nonetheless, some strands of contemporary transnational feminisms are related to the neoliberal lobby that appropriates feminist discourse to justify conservative, racist, and imperialist arguments. On the other hand, we find the trans-excluding movement, whose main argument is to essentialize cis-women as the only subject of feminism, excluding from feminism everyone who does not conform to its model of biological womanhood. It is important to highlight that the goal of this text is not to deny the predatory violence suffered today and historically by cis-gender women inside hetero-necro-patriarchy. On the contrary, we recognize this violence, and we know that it is not haphazard but part of the binary gender structure. Thus, the present text places the need to form alliances between cis and trans women to create strategies of common resistance against it.

That is why it is urgent to place ourselves, coming from different feminisms, as a common front, since, as Audre Lorde (1983: 99) set forth, "Without community, there is no liberation"; moreover, without community there is only "the most vulnerable and temporary armistice between an individual and her oppression." In this regard, it is necessary to resume the project of creating the common good, which considers that "community must not mean a shedding of our differences, nor the pathetic pretense that these differences do not exist" (99). On the contrary, the creation of a *sumak kawsay* is based on an attitude of self-criticism and redefinition where the different political issues that have preoccupied earlier iterations of feminisms are put on the table, such as equal rights and access to citizenship, as well as new forms of feminisms that are more attentive to everyday sexism, femicide, harassment, and violence on social media, and multimodal violence.[6] In this context, transfeminism emerges as a movement centered on the destigmatization of sex work, the depathologization of trans people, and the expansion of the political subjects of feminism, intersectionality, and decoloniality.

The call of transfeminisms is to perform a self-criticism that does not exclude as subjects of feminism those who "stand outside the circle of this society's definition of acceptable women; those of us who have been forged in the crucibles of difference; those of who are poor, who are lesbian, who are black, who are older" (Lorde 1983: 99); who are indigenous, who are trans, who do not participate in the Western aesthetic canon, who have functional diversity, who are refugees, migrants, undocumented, precarious, "who speak in tongues" (Anzaldúa 1988: 219); who precisely because of their subjectifying and desubjectifying intersections participate in the physical, psychological, and medial consequences brought by the growing globalization of explicitly morbid, that is, the gore violence that has real effects on trans and cis-gender women's lives.

Transfeminism is more than a dissenting gesture or the adoption of a certain aesthetics and prosthetics, tied to the gender performances represented by queer theory, since it appeals to the construction of a social and political common front that renders account of the violence established and naturalized artificially as a "narrative strategy that is deliberately fractured" (Villaplana and Sichel 2005: 269), that concerns all the discursive fields and that can be identified, with special vigor, in the way the media represents sexist violence. Transfeminism as a political front positions itself in "the defense of the anti-normative and anti-assimilationist practices and experiences" (Flores 2017: 37) to de-necropoliticize our existence.

Necropolitics, Neopolitics, and Postmortem/Transmortem Politics in the Sexual Economies of Death

I take the term *necropolitics* from the Cameroonian theoretician Achille Mbembe (2012: 136), who defines it as "the type of politics where this is understood as the labour of death in the production of a world where the limits of death are finished." Mbembe uses this concept to refer to three questions addressed (1) "to the contexts where the state of emergency has become normal;" (2) "to the figures of sovereignty whose main project is the generalized instrumentalization of human existence and the material destruction of the bodies and human populations judged as disposable or redundant"; and (3) "to the figures of sovereignty where power or government refer or appeal continuously to emergency and to a fictionalized or phantasmal vision of the enemy. All of this as a way of ending with the idea of prohibiting widespread killing, that because we are under the threat, we can kill without distinction whoever we consider to be our enemy" (135).

I use Mbembe's definition of necropolitics as a reference point to talk about violence as a link between the colonial and the contemporary project of modernity through the systematic and continuous elimination of dissenting populations. In this sense, it is important to expand the scope of the term *necropolitics* beyond race and class to the governability of cis and trans women and those others that embody dissenting genders and sexualities, such as trans masculinities, that defy the hetero norm and the binary *cis-tem*, thus being produced in the collective imaginary as aberrant populations that may/must be demarcated as enemies to be brutally and violently destroyed.

In this sense, I propose necropolitics as the management and capitalization of the death processes that are highly tied to sexism and necropatriarchy in the Mexican state. Necropolitical power expands in a metastable way, among classes, races and generations, regularly leading against those who are nonbinary, queer, racialized, poor, renegade, and/or people living in conditions of precarity.[7]

I understand necropatriarchy as the privilege of exercising the techniques of necropolitical violence proffered by the patriarchy to the figure-body of the individual man (as microsovereign of the populations in his charge). So men have among their gender privileges the knowledge and cultural socialization in the use of the techniques of necropolitics, and legitimacy in the handling and use of violence as a key technique of rule. That is, in case of the Mexican patriarchal pact, as in many similar arrangements, the executors of violence, usually heterosexual cis men, act as armed soldiers of the "sovereign." Their crimes occur with impunity, and there is a persistent lack of justice for trans and cis women, as well as minority populations. Due to their race/ethnicity, sexuality, and class, they possess a monopoly over the techniques of death, ruling over gender, class, race, sexual dissent, and functional diversity.

The most visible face of this necropatriarchy is the (trans)femicidal machine that up to this day accounts for more than 53,000 femicides committed against women from 1985 to 2016 in the Mexican territory (Echarri Cánovas 2017).[8]

I use the concept of neopolitics to define the occupation of a political field populated by minoritarian becomings that do not hoist a common flag but that apparently debate with their presence "an embodied claim for a more livable life" (Butler 2015: 119), that is, a demand of public intersectional dignification, that appropriates the right to speak and appear in public: to do politics. But it is a politics that does not call on the simple representation/representativeness that articulates under the old binary mandates of the male sovereignty understood, and whose common cause leaves out of the democratic frame the intersections and the differences since they defy "the technological construction of the 'natural truth' of the sexes that is done with the support of a binary and visual epistemological regime of the hetero-centered conception of the human" (Flores 2017: 35). On the contrary, under a multiplicity of demands that configure a political constellation that cannot be subsumed to the neoliberal ideals of normalization, this neopolitics presents itself with multiple faces and geopolitics that speak in tongues (Anzaldúa 1988) and not only in the official protest language. This multitude seeks for other interlocutors to make practical alliances to avoid enclosure, dispossession, and the massacre.

In this sense, transfeminisms are forms of this neopolitics, since they aspire not to become citizens-consumers but to transit through other nonbinary circuits where the agendas of insurrection do not put identitarian or national limits.[9] On the contrary, they make us share practices of dissent, survival, and interdependence in the face of the unrestrained massacre of necroliberalism.

Transpolitics emerges as a radical epistemic paradigm shift of the traditional definition of the political, where survival strategies appeal to the disobedience of established rules to be "good savages" and "good minorities" by reworking embodiment with the "body present" the lexicon of insubordination,[10] thereby making possible the reorganization of the political from little traveled areas in spaces where vulnerability and damage to the bodies of women and nonbinary people and injustice are the norm.[11]

The Case of Paola Sánchez Romero, Example of Postmortem/Transmortem Politics

Sarah Nuttall (2012) asks: "How and in what terms do we go back to the question about the dead body now, as a body, mourned life and form of mortality, desert and void in the political body?" (93). I contemplate the possibility of answering from a transfeminist framework that seeks to name death not only as an act that closes and deletes life but also as a process that happens in stages inside the continuous massacre that many minoritarian populations experience. It isn't my intention to deny the fact that murder radically cuts life; however, before this radical denial and appalling privatization, political responses have arisen, using the presentation of the dead body to dignify it and avoid its erasure. It is this mobilization of the murdered and present body that I call *postmortem/transmortem politics*.

In the early morning of September 30, 2016, in the Puente de Alvarado Avenue, in Mexico City, Paola Sánchez Romero, a trans woman, was murdered while working. The murderer, Arturo Delgadillo, the alleged armed escort of a public official from Naucalpan, asked for her sexual services and a few minutes after twenty-seven-year-old Paola got in his car, he shot her twice in the heart.

The facts were told by her coworkers, who ran to her rescue on hearing the gunshots. The killer was captured by the sex workers and handed over to the police, who transferred him to the offices of the Fiscalía Desconcentrada en Investigación (Decentralized Prosecutors Office of Investigation) in the Cuauhtémoc Delegation, where Kenya, one of the trans women who witnessed the events, recognized him and also the gun he wielded that night: a 9mm Pietro Beretta. However, despite having overwhelming evidence and eye-witness accounts, the judge, Gilberto Cervantes Hernández, set the murderer free on October 2, 2016, two days after the arrest, arguing that there wasn't evidence enough to incriminate Delgadillo (Gilet 2016).

After the exculpatory sentence, Paola's friends wondered during her funeral, Where is the justice for those that cannot pay for it? Their question poses an accurate critique of the Mexican state, where law and justice are not the same thing—on the contrary, where the state and its agents claim the power to apply the law discretionally, or not apply it at all. Paola's friends decided not to resign themselves in the face of this injustice, and on the way to the cemetery, they removed their dead friend's body from the coffin at the site of the murder, as a protest and call for justice. This justice is no longer being claimed only from the state; rather, it is a call for others to empathize with the rage and impotence generated in the Mexican population by the inattention and the lack of follow-up of crimes and all type of offences, especially the ones committed against trans and cis women, which lead to daily transfemicides and femicides (*El Gráfico* 2016; Cultura Diversa 2016). In this context, this community of trans sex workers decided to display their dead friend's body to call for the production of an alliance, even if it is an spontaneous one.

They decided not to stay only in the obituaries or accept these as the only legal and allowed way in the modern West to manifest their mourning. On the contrary, they displayed a postmortem/transmortem politics that refutes, transgresses, and disobeys necropower, since, as Martín De Mauro Rucovsky (2017: 154) reflects, "what necropower achieves, and the corresponding femicidal violence, is to dislocate the 'sepulchral pact,' inasmuch it destroys the ties of that body with the community."

So the objective of the politics of the present (dead) body, that is, postmortem/transmortem, activated by the act of this community of trans Mexican women in answer to Paola's transfemicide, is precisely the rearticulation of the strength of the community for "re-construction of a biographical frame of (trans)femicidal violence in dispute with the judicial-police narrative and also the journalistic chronicles written from ontological presuppositions that were individualizing and personalistic [and stigmatizing]" (De Mauro Rucovsky 2017: 151).

This act of displaying a dead body is the inverse of the exhibition and trashification of the bodies of the women killed violently in a femicide done by the media.[12] This dignified act of displaying a dead body nullifies its disappearance, its oblivion; it rebels against the indifference toward another death, prohibits mutism, and forces estrangement, since as B. Ianina Moretti (2017: 26) argues, "the bodily exhibition enables alliances, illuminates an interdependence that allows agencies that challenge this normative violence." This act, organized from worthy rage, can be considered spontaneous, minimum and isolated, but its occurrence in fact moves the structures of Mexican social anesthesia around (trans)femicide, since society has become used to daily counting dead cis and trans women at the hands of necropatriarchal violence.

Thus, this demonstration against the corruption of the justice system displays a political dimension that transgresses the nominalist regulations, giving voice and body to other forms of struggle and resistance, even after death, exemplifying cruelly and starkly the conditions in which certain trans populations live and die every day. Beyond a visibilization of the murder and the impunity, the act of displaying Paola's body after its death inaugurates a displacement of the exercise of the political through postmortem/transmortem politics.

This postmortem politics manages to overcome the saturation of spectacle and trivialization of dead bodies, challenging the official visual narrative produced around femicide and the political, where a fragmented narrative is portrayed, where violence is not assumed as inattention or a breach of the state commitments to guarantee the security and protection of the populations the state is in charge of, and where the media revictimizes or disqualifies the facts, blaming the murdered women through moral judgments about their sexuality, their gender, and their class.

This gesture of transmortem activism shifts the scope of collective agency, positioning itself as a methodology of mourning from agency and from the construction of a memory that does not revictimize. This act calls out for the mobilization of communities and alliances where the transpolitical not only circumscribes to living bodies but also claims alliance with the murdered bodies, dead bodies, and disappeared bodies that integrate the necropolitical and grieving map of contemporary Mexico.

In this sense, the political body of transfeminisms is characterized by making strategic alliances that exceed the limits of traditional politics. These alliances articulate a complex social ontology; that is, they unify coherently a social body in constant modification, which constructs performatively an ethics and a politics that suspend the emotional precariousness, dignifying life. In this way, Transfeminisms enable the construction of a memory that is still fragile but not peremptory.

A memory where postmortem/transmortem politics represent an unsettling act that changes the rules of the game and of decoding violence against us: queer people. This postmortem memory breaks the pacts with the language of grieving imposed by the sexual elite and its promises of safety and well-being for all, which are the basis of contemporary democracies.

Finally, this deeply disobeying and intricately political gesture links transpolitics to a dissenting way of production of signs, syntax, languages, and what is involved in the process of subjectivation and the ways of producing and reproducing life in an extremely violent context. The presentation of a dead body is an interruption of the social anesthesia in the face of the ever-present massacre, producing affective answers that modify the structures of social perception about trans people and the minoritarian becomings as worthy and with a right to live. It is also inspiring, inasmuch as they are capable of gaining agency from unexpected political imaginations, creating routes and maneuvers to act and appear in a way that is not comparable to the logics of normalizing-devouring of institutional politics.

Conclusions

In this article I have reflected about the postmortem/transmortem politics executed by a Mexican trans community that, in displaying the murdered body of one of their community members, exceeds the limits of the political in its traditional sense. With this action, the surviving women of this community become trans Antigones.[13] They refuse to obey or transit through the circuits of conventional political claims because Paola is all of us, because she is saying from the afterlife: "I do not want to die this death" (Mbembe 2016). The postmortem politics is this "present body" that comes back to challenge the visual anesthesia that is produced by the mediation and reproduction of the catastrophe and the (trans)femicide through mass media and cultural devices linked to reproducing sexist, chauvinist, racist, heteronormed, and necropatriarcal narratives and values.

Sayak Valencia, also known as Margarita Valencia Triana, holds a PhD in philosophy from the Universidad Complutense de Madrid, is a feminist theoretician and critic, and is a member of the National System of Researchers in Mexico (level 1). She is a tenured professor and researcher at the Department of Cultural Studies of El Colegio de la Frontera Norte, research center CONACYT, Mexico. Her research areas are feminisms, transfeminisms, violence, drug trafficking and capitalism, and queer/*cuir* and decolonial studies. She is the author of *Gore Capitalism* (2018).

Acknowledgments

I thank Claudia Sofía Garriga-López for her extensive editorial assistance and generous contributions to the form and substance of this article.

Notes

1. I take inspiration from Félix Guattari and Suely Rolnik's (2006) perspective, which defines *minoritarian becomings* as a process that does not essentialize the identities but is performative; that is, one is not essentially minoritarian but becomes so because of gender, race, class, sexual orientation, functional diversity, migration status, and so forth, such as becoming black, becoming woman, or becoming migrant. However, the potential

of these becomings translates not to a passive reproduction of subalternization but to the creation of other imageries and political potencies that build queer alternatives that create networks of affection and survival in highly normative and violent contexts.

2.   Given the length and approach of the article, it focuses on the reflection about transfeminist connections between cis and transgender women besieged by femicide. However, this does not mean that I do not consider it important to think about the connection of transfeminism with transmasculine people. I suggest consulting important transmasculine thinkers that have addressed this topic, such as Paul Preciado (2018) and Jack Halberstam (1998).

3.   "*Cuir* represents an *ostranienie* (de-familiarization) of the term *queer*, that is, a de-automation of the reading glance, and it registers the geopolitical inflection towards the South and from the peripheries as a counteroffensive to the colonial epistemology and the Anglo-American historiography. Thus, the movement from *queer* to *cuir* refers to a locus of enunciation with a decolonial inflection, both playful and critical" (Valencia 2015: 34).

4.   The queer perspective considers that the process of standardization/normalization of sexed bodies in a gender-binary categorization is violent in itself, hence the term *gender-based violence*, not *gender violence*.

5.   I use the term *necro-neoliberalism* to talk about the use of necropolitical techniques applied by the capitalist neoliberal regime to generate economic, political, or social capital, through violence and death, which in other works I have called gore capitalism (Valencia 2018).

6.   In Andean communities in Latin America, development is expressed through the notion of *sumak kawsay*, the Quechua word for *buen vivir*, "good living," or "living well." *Sumak kawsay* has been proposed as an alternative conception of development and has been incorporated into the constitutions of Ecuador and *suma qamaña* (*vivir bien*) in Bolivia. It connotes a harmonious collective development that conceives of the individual within the context of the social and cultural communities and his or her natural environment (Houtart 2011).

7.   Celia Amorós (1994: 27) defines this pact as follows: "Patriarchy could be considered as a kind of interclass, metastable agreement that becomes the heritage of the generic of the males, who institute themselves as the subjects of the social contract against women, who are the 'agreed.' Said like this, it is very schematic. . . . But normally patriarchy would be this—interclass—pact by which power constitutes itself as the heritage of the generic of males. In this pact, of course, the covenant parties are not in equal conditions, because there are different classes, and those class differences are not irrelevant. But it should be remembered, as Heidi Hartmann very appropriately does, that the family wage is a patriarchal pact among males of antagonistic social classes to socially control women."

8.   I take the term *femicidal machine* from the Mexican writer and journalist Sergio González Rodríguez, who suggests it to analyze the femicide in Ciudad Juárez in his book *Huesos en el desierto*, published in 2002, and reedited in 2005 by the Barcelonian press house Anagrama.

9.   The term *transfeminism* seeks to enunciate a critical update of the traditional way of interpreting and managing the sex-gender system and the sexuality that affect the political subject of feminism. That is, transfeminism puts in the center of the debate the need to articulate intersectionally the heterosexual norm as a political and economic regime that unleashes the sexual division of labor and originates the structural inequalities between the genders, crossed by specificities of race/ethnicity, class, and

sexual dissent with new elements, such as the nonexclusion and the depathologization of trans bodies, the legalization of sex work, the reappropriation of pornographic representation (feminist postpornography), the critique of romantic love, functional diversity, and the body-decolonial critique of the fat power movement, as well as the intensive violence where the dissenting bodies are located in highly neoliberalized and/or excolonial countries. This incorporation of elements to the feminist agendas has been claimed for more than a decade by different activist collectives in Latin America and Spain; to mention only a few, in Spain, Guerrilla travolaka (guerrilla-travolaka.blogspot.com), Colectivo Hetaira (www.colectivohetaira.org), and Post Op (archivo-t.net/post-op/), and thinkers/writers/artists such as Paul Preciado (2009), Itziar Ziga (2009), Diana J. Torres (2011), and Miriam Solá and Elena Urko (2013); in Ecuador, Ana Almeida and Eli Vázquez (2010); in my own Mexico, (Valencia 2010, 2012, 2014; Valencia and Sepúlveda 2016); in Argentina, Laura Milano (2014) and Nicolás Cuello and Laura Contrera (2016); in Chile, Colectivo CUDS (disidenciasexualcuds.wordpress.com/about/); in Colombia, Nadia Granados "La Fulminante"(www.lafulminante.com).

10.   I am referencing the two meanings of the Spanish expression *de cuerpo presente*, which, on the one hand, refers to a living person, someone who is really present, not through a representative or otherwise; on the other hand, it also references a corpse, which is exposed and ready to be taken after the burial.

11.   I use the term *gore capitalism* (Valencia 2010) to reference the reinterpretation given to hegemonic and global economy in (geographically) border spaces, where the processes of giving death are more visibly capitalized.

12.   On this topic, you can review the contributions of such feminist theoreticians as Rita Segato (2003), Mariana Berlanga (2018), and Julia Monárrez (2009).

13.   With this metaphor, I am linking the act of transmortem politics and the story of Antigone, a character from Greek mythology who disobeys the order of King Creon, who prohibits her to give a proper burial to her dead brother. In the myth, Antigone transgresses the prohibition and buries her brother with the proper funeral ceremonies of the Greeks, and because of it, she is condemned to death. However, with this disregard, Antigone creates a new ethical parameter above blind obedience to authority, establishing a frame of political action that privileges the value of dignity and affection above laws based on authoritarianism and injustice.

References

Almeida, Ana, and Elizabeth Vásquez, eds. 2013. *Cuerpos Distintos: Ocho años de activismo transfeminista en Ecuador.* Quito: Comisión de Transición Consejo Nacional de las Mujeres y la Igualdad de Género.

Amorós, Celia. 1994. *Feminismo: Igualdad y diferencia.* Mexico City: Programa Universitario de Estudios de Género, Universidad Nacional Autónoma de México.

Anzaldúa, Gloria. 1988. "Hablar en lenguas: Una carta a escritoras tercermundistas." In *Esta puente mi espalda: Voces de mujeres tercermundistas en los Estados Unidos*, edited by Cherríe Moraga and Ana Castillo, 219–30. San Francisco: Ism Press.

Berlanga, Mariana. 2018. *Una mirada al feminicidio.* Mexico City: Ítaca / Universidad Autónoma de la Ciudad de México.

Butler, Judith. 1993. *Bodies That Matter: On the Discursive Limits of "Sex."* New York: Routledge.

Butler, Judith. 2017. 2015. *Notes towards a Performative Theory of Assembly.* Cambridge, MA: Harvard University Press.

Cuello, Nicolás, and Laura Contrera. 2016. *Cuerpos sin patrones: Resistencias desde las geografías desmesuradas de la carne*. Buenos Aires: Madreselva.

Cultura Diversa. 2016. "Exigen justicia para Paola por trans feminicidio." October 5. www.youtube .com/watch?v=fkXAFnA5SEE

De Mauro Rucovsky, Martín. 2017. "0,1 notas sobre ¿cómo leer un caso de feminicidio?" In *¿Qué hacemos con las normas que nos hacen? Usos de Judith Butler*, edited by Alberto Canseco, María Victoria Dahbar, amd Emma Song, 147–73. Córdoba, Argentina: Sexualidades Doctas.

Echarri Cánovas, Carlos Javier. 2017. *La violencia feminicida en México, aproximaciones y tendencias 1985–2016*. México Secretaría de Gobernación, Instituto Nacional de las Mujeres, y Entidad de las Naciones Unidas para la Igualdad de Género y el Empoderamiento de las Mujeres. www.gob.mx/cms/uploads/attachment/file/293666/violenciaFeminicidaMx _07dic_web.pdf.

El Gráfico. 2016. "Amigos y familiares de trabajadora asesinada se manifiestan en Insurgentes y Puente de Alvarado." October 4. www.youtube.com/watch?v=sE33z7neF0Q.

Fernández-Savater, Amador, Pablo Lapuente Tiana, and Amarela Varela. 2016. "Achille Mbembe: 'Cuando el poder brutaliza el cuerpo, la resistencia asume una forma visceral.'" *El Diario*, June 17. www.eldiario.es/interferencias/Achille-Mbembe-brutaliza-resistencia-visceral _6_527807255.html.

Flores, Valeria. 2017. *Tropismos de la disidencia*. Santiago, Chile: Editorial Palinodia, Colección Archivo Feminista.

Garriga-López, Claudia Sofía. 2019. "Transfeminism." In *Global Encyclopedia of Lesbian, Gay, Bisexual, Transgender, and Queer (LGBTQ) History*, edited by Howard Chiang. Farmington Hills, MI: Scribner's.

Gilet, Eliana. 2016. "Paola, la chica trans asesinada impunemente en la CDMX." *Vice*, December 17. www.vice.com/es_latam/article/bn4w7v/la-historia-completa-de-paola-transexual -asesinada-impune-prostituta.

González Rodríguez, Sergio. 2005. *Huesos en el desierto*. Barcelona: Anagrama.

Guattari, Félix, and Suely Rolnik. 2006. *Micropolítica: Cartografías del deseo*. Madrid: Traficantes de Sueños.

Halberstam, Jack. 1998. *Female Masculinity*. Durham, NC: Duke University Press.

Houtart, François. 2011. "El concepto de *sumak kawsai* (buen vivir) y su correspondencia con el bien común de la humanidad." *Alai-Amlatina*, June 2. www.alainet.org/es/active/47004.

Kanter, Rosabeth M. 1977. *Men and Women of the Corporation*. New York: Basic Books.

Kauanui, Kēhaulani. 2016. "'A Structure, Not an Event': Settler Colonialism and Enduring Indigeneity." *Lateral* 5, no. 1. csalateral.org/issue/5-1/forum-alt-humanities-settler-colonialism -enduring-indigeneity-kauanui/.

Lorde, Audre. 1983. "The Master's Tools Will Never Dismantle the Master's House." In *This Bridge Called My Back: Writing from Radical Women of Color*, 2nd ed., edited by Cherrie Moraga and Gloria Anzaldúa, 98–101. New York: Kitchen Table.

Lugones, María. 2008. "Colonialidad y género." *Tabula Rasa*, no. 9: 75–101.

Milano, Laura. 2014. *Usina posporno: Disidencia sexual, arte y autogestión en la pospornografía*. Buenos Aires: Editorial Título.

Mbembe, Achille. 2012. "Necropolítica: Una revisión crítica." In *Estética y violencia: Necropolítica, militarización y vidas lloradas*, edited by Elena Chávez McGregor, 131–37. Mexico City: Museo Universitario de Arte Contemporáneo / Universidad Nacional Autónoma de México.

Mbembe, Achille, 2016. "Cuando el poder brutaliza el cuerpo, la resistencia asume una forma visceral." Interview with Amador Fernández-Savater, Pablo Lapuente Tiana, and Amarela Varela. *El Diario*, June 17. www.eldiario.es/interferencias/Achille-Mbembe -brutaliza-resistencia-visceral_6_527807255.html.

Monárrez, Julia. 2009. *Trama de una injusticia: Feminicidio sexual sistémico en Ciudad Juárez*. Mexico City: El Colegio de la Frontera Norte / Miguel Ángel Porrúa.

Moretti, B. Ianina. 2017. "Juego de heraldos: La pregunta por la agencia." In *¿Qué hacemos con las normas que nos hacen? Usos de Judith Butler*, edited by Alberto Canseco, María Victoria Dahbar, and Emma Song, 23–47. Córdoba, Argentina: Sexualidades Doctas.

Muedano, Marcos. 2017. "Imparable, el crimen contra las mujeres; cifras del Inegi." *Excélsior*, October 22. www.excelsior.com.mx/nacional/2017/10/22/1196308.

Nuttall, Sarah. 2012. "Violencia, re-composición, superficie: Culturas visuales en Johannesburgo." In *Estética y violencia: Necropolítica, militarización y vidas lloradas*, edited by Elena Chávez McGregor, 93–115. Mexico City: Museo Universitario de Arte Contemporáneo / Universidad Nacional Autónoma de México.

Preciado, Paul. 2018. "#MeToo: Carta de un hombre trans al antiguo régimen sexual." *Ara en Castellano*, January 28. www.ara.cat/es/opinion/Paul-B-Preciado-Carta-hombre-trans -antiguo-regimen-sexual_0_1951605023.html.

Preciado, Paul. 2009. "Transfeminismos y micropolíticas del género en la era farmacopornográfica." *Revista Artecontexto*, no. 21: 58–61.

Proyecto Transrespeto versus Transfobia en el Mundo. 2017. "Día de la memoria trans 2017." Transrespect, November 14. transrespect.org/es/tmm-update-trans-day-remembrance-2017.

Segato, Rita Laura. 2003. "Las estructuras elementales de la violencia: Contrato y estatus en la etimología de la violencia." *Série Antropologia* (Departamento de Antropología, Brasília) 334: 14–15.

Solá, Miriam, and Elena Urko, eds. 2013. *Transfeminismos: Epistemes, fricciones y flujos*. Navarra: Txlaparta.

Torres, Diana. 2011. *Pornoterrorismo*. Navarra: Txlaparta.

Valencia, Sayak. 2010. *Capitalismo gore*. Barcelona: Melusina.

Valencia, Sayak. 2012. "Capitalismo gore y necropolítica en México contemporáneo." *Relaciones Internacionales*, no. 19: 83–102.

Valencia, Sayak. 2014. "Teoría transfeminista para el análisis de la violencia machista y la recon-strucción del tejido social en México contemporáneo." *Universitas Humanística*, no. 78: 65–88.

Valencia, Sayak. 2015. "Del queer al cuir: Ostranénie geopolítica y epistémica desde el sur g-local." In *Queer y cuir: Políticas de lo irreal*, edited by Fernando R. Lanuza and Raúl M. Carrasco, 19–37. Mexico City: Editorial Fontamara.

Valencia, Sayak. 2018. *Gore Capitalism*. Pasadena, CA: Semiotext(e).

Valencia, Sayak, and Katia Sepúlveda. 2016. "Del Fascinante Fascismo a la fascinante violencia: Psico/bio/necro/política y mercado gore." *Mitologías hoy*, no. 14: 75–91.

Villaplana, Virginia, and Berta Sichel. 2005. *Cárcel de amor: Relatos culturales en torno a la violencia de género*. Madrid: Museo Nacional Centro de Arte Reina Sofía.

Wolfe, Patrick. 1999. *Settler Colonialism and the Transformation of Anthropology: The Politics and Poetics of an Ethnographic Event*. London: Cassell.

Ziga, Itziar. 2009. *Devenir Perra*. Barcelona: Editorial Melusina.

Antitrans State Terrorism
Trans and Travesti Women, Human Rights, and Recent History in Chile

HILLARY HINER and JUAN CARLOS GARRIDO

Translated by BRIGETTE WALTERS

Abstract This article analyzes the ways in which trans and *travesti* women experienced state terrorism during the Chilean military dictatorship (1973–90), a subject that has received little attention in memory and recent history studies in Chile. In particular, the authors propose that the use of the concept of human rights by truth commissions, as well as its inclusion in public policies, has largely excluded trans and travesti women. This text therefore introduces the concept of antitrans state terrorism and, given the limited studies that exist on the subject, encourages more historiographic research of state terrorism and trans and travesti women in Chile.

Keywords trans and travesti women, antitrans state terrorism, human rights, recent history, Chile

Introduction: State Terrorism, Human Rights, and Trans/Travesti Studies

Why have trans and *travesti* women been excluded from discourses on state terrorism, human rights, and memory in Chile?[1] Several factors contribute to this historical oversight. First, while there has been a growing and important interest in women, sexual political violence, and memory in Latin America (Arfuch 2013; Hiner 2009; Jelin 2001), such interest rarely applies to trans women or LGBTQI-related issues. Moreover, while from a historiographic perspective James Green (1999, 2012) has worked extensively with these topics, his work focuses on Brazil and considers male homosexuality, queer militants in left-wing armed groups, political violence against those groups, and forms of resisting such violence. Finally, while various trans and travesti women activists have denounced the violence of the civic-military dictatorship in Chile, such as Claudia Rodríguez and the trans advocacy group Organizing Trans Diversities (Organizando Trans Diversidades, OTD), these efforts have not been officially recognized by the Chilean state. Thus, while previous works and efforts are of undeniable importance, our

TSQ: Transgender Studies Quarterly ★ Volume 6, Number 2 ★ May 2019 **194**
DOI 10.1215/23289252-7348482 © 2019 Duke University Press

research is innovative in that it analyzes, from a historical perspective, another type of state terrorism: that which was directed toward trans and travesti women during the military dictatorship in Chile (1973–90).

It is important to remember that the trans and travesti community in Chile experiences violence in many ways, from the structural and symbolic violence that is gender assignment and subsequent efforts to modify this gender to the daily economic, physical, psychological, and sexual violence that trans people face both from strangers and those close to them. This is what Lohana Berkins (2003: 151) points to when she argues that "travesti people are under siege daily. The routine persecution by police, the everyday inability to move freely through the streets performing a subversive identity, and the permanent obstacles to accessing the rights guaranteed to all citizens, among other things, these make the travesti life one under constant siege."[2] As such, state terrorism can be considered one more type of violence experienced by many of the trans and travesti women interviewed. Following Judith Butler's (2006) work on the murder of trans people like Brandon Teena and Gwen Araujo, we also hold that trans and travesti women who experienced state terrorism in Chile are worthy of mourning and public recognition and are included in the *human* in *human rights*. From our perspective, historiography has an important role in recognizing the state terrorism carried out against trans and travesti women in Chile. More specifically, the ways in which this violence and its effects persist into the present, as well as how trans and travesti women and their organizations have come to resist these continuities, must be considered.

In this article, we primarily consider violence against trans and travesti women during the Chilean dictatorship and refer therein to a concept we call *antitrans state terrorism.*[3] We use this term to refer to acts of authoritarian oppression and torture—referred to as *state terrorism* in Latin America—and to emphasize the official state role of the violence (see, e.g., Dinges 2004; Feierstein 2009) committed against trans and travesti people—mostly women—during the dictatorship. Calling this type of violence *antitrans* allows for the identification and documentation of dictatorial crimes committed specifically against trans people. This type of violence often results in death, a crime that in nondictatorial cases is referred to as *trans-femicide* or *travesticide* (Radi and Sardpa-Chandiramani 2016).

Some studies of antitrans state terrorism have considered hate crimes against trans and travesti people in Brazil. For example, many were detained and forced to clean the police stations or police vehicles or even wash bodies in the morgue, jobs that were considered "female" tasks and meant to humiliate and terrorize (Mott 1996: 35). Studies of the Argentine dictatorship take a slightly different view, maintaining that state repression of LGBTQI people was primarily a result of the homophobia of the police officers and prison guards themselves, since, at the time, there was no specific program that sought to police sexual dissidence. That is to say, the political violence in these cases did not have the objective of persecuting gay, lesbian, or trans people and thus entails a type of political violence distinct from antitrans violence (Insausti 2015: 73). There are also studies that emphasize the clandestine nature of queer culture under Latin American dictatorships, both to make possible spaces for homoerotic experiences and to avoid police control over "public morality" (Figari 2009: 167). Finally, and more in line with the present study, there is research on the murder of trans and travesti women by death squads that sought to eliminate homosexual, lesbian, and trans/travesti groups during dictatorships, such as the Escuadrón Hortela in Brazil (Mott 1996) and the Comando Cóndor and Comando Moralidad in Argentina (Figari 2010).

In the particular case of Chile, there have been a handful of studies on dictatorial violence against trans and travesti women, including the work of Víctor Hugo Robles (2008), Óscar Contardo (2012), and Juan Carlos Garrido (2016). Garrido uses oral history to analyze the violence enacted through article 373 of the Chilean Criminal Code, which penalizes "any significant or scandalous offense against decency or good behavior." Although this article of the Criminal Code has been used in both dictatorial and democratic contexts to prosecute women doing street sex work, the lack of oversight by a rule of law during the dictatorship resulted in its much more arbitrary and violent application against trans and travesti women. Consequently, transphobic oppression was multifaceted, including street violence, sexual violence, homicide, criminalization, and constant harassment from both the police and the public. The lack of official recognition of antitrans state terrorism during the dictatorship, specifically toward trans and travesti women, hinders the creation of reparative policies, as well as the advancement of LGBTQI rights in a time when there is already little interest in exploring this violent past. Thus, this article presents a new perspective for recent history studies in Chile: antitrans violence committed during the military dictatorship and described through the testimonies of the trans and travesti women who experienced it directly.

Debates on Recent History and LGBTQI Studies in Chile

Texts about recent history and memory in Chile tend to share several characteristics. First, these fields are dominated by historians and academics from the social sciences who focus their analyses on the period between 1964 (the election of Eduardo Frei Montalva) or 1970 (the election of Salvador Allende) and 1990, when Patricio Aylwin assumed the presidency and the dictatorship of Augusto Pinochet was formally ended. This period is generally seen as a "rupture," the dictatorship bursting forth and eradicating a democratic tradition that would eventually return in 1990. While many studies have questioned this so-called return to democracy, given the neoliberal continuities between the dictatorship and the Concertación (Coalition of Parties for Democracy) in the 1990s, they have nevertheless failed to question the exclusion of certain historical subjects such as trans and travesti people, indigenous peoples, Afro-descendants, and shantytown or peasant women, all of whom have been left out of constructs of democracy and citizenship following the dictatorship. Second, studies of recent history and memory tend to be androcentric and heterosexist, particularly those produced in Chile. One explanation for this is that studies of the Holocaust and the civic-military dictatorships of the Southern Cone are already thirty or more years old and thus do not reflect more recent gender and sexuality turns. Violence is considered largely in terms of the political violence of authoritarianism, such as forced disappearances and torture, and makes little reference to violence having to do with gender or sexuality. Finally, texts that break from androcentrism and use gender theory almost exclusively reference heterosexual cis women, limiting their research and theorization to the paradigm of women's history or *grandes mujeres* (extraordinary women), both of which derive from second-wave feminism. Although these studies are without a doubt valuable, they exclude from their analyses the experiences of trans and travesti women affected by antitrans state terrorism. These women were not militants of political parties and therefore did not experience "political violence," nor did they, generally, undergo the typical sequence of human rights violations at the time (i.e., abduction, torture in a secret detention center, forced disappearance).

How might we consider a trans historiography of Chile that accounts for state terrorism? What are the possible lines of investigation? There are many possibilities for approaching and writing a trans history of state terrorism during the dictatorship. The present investigation uses oral histories and ethnography to explore the historical experiences of trans and travesti women in Chile and consider how their stories can contribute to recent history and memory studies. The women interviewed cover a wide age range, born between 1956 and 1994. The interviews were completed in various regions of the country, but with most done in the north (Arica and Parinacota, Tarapacá, and Antofagasta regions) and Santiago. Most of the interviewees were activists in their respective communities, in the form of involvement with LGBTQI groups, political parties, or student groups. Many of the women participated in groups dedicated specifically to trans and travesti issues, like Nefertiti in Iquique, Arcoiris in Antofagasta and, in Santiago, groups like OTD, Transítar, Traves Chile, and the travesti sex workers' union, the Amanda Jofré Union.

Interestingly, the gender identities of those interviewed varied without much overlap. These included, among others, transgender woman, *trava* or travesti, trans woman, transfeminine, transsexual female, transgender (without a *man* or *woman* signifier), and gender fluid. Sexuality was also discussed, and the interviewees mentioned if they preferred dating cis men or cis women, sometimes taking on labels according to more traditional categories, like *gay* or *hetero*. *Bi* and *pan* identities were often referenced when no preference or a preference for both was given, *pan* being more common with younger people.

The current demands of trans groups in Chile were also brought up in the interviews, such as the Gender Identity Law, recently passed by the Chilean Congress in September 2018, the improvement of the antidiscrimination law (known as the Zamudio Law and named for a hate crime committed against Daniel Zamudio, a young gay man murdered in Santiago in 2012), and, more generally, the absence of the state in trans and travesti matters. The following testimonies are excerpts taken from much longer and much more violent accounts. Ellipses (…) are used in some cases to avoid the inclusion of explicit details about the torture of trans bodies. This decision is aligned with a larger ethical debate within trans studies that endeavors to avoid the overrepresentation of tortured trans bodies and to respect the dignity of those interviewed.[4]

Oral History and Antitrans State Terrorism

Article 373 of the Chilean Criminal Code condemned offenses to decency, morality, and good behavior, a vestige of nineteenth-century ecclesiastical ideas that sought to discourage the fostering of moral decadence in Western society (Hopman 2000). The vague wording of the law left it free to be interpreted by the authorities and, as a result, allowed for the constant harassment of trans and travesti groups and justified various police raids on gay bars and clubs, as well as sex work zones. While antitrans violence certainly existed previously in Chile (e.g., during the government of Carlos Ibáñez del Campo and the Popular Unity government), the military dictatorship intensified the repression of trans and travesti women with article 373 and the abuse of power at the hands of both the Carabineros (Chilean national police force) and parts of Chilean society.[5] At the same time, the situation of trans and travesti women during the 1970s and 1980s was already complex. Many of the interviewees mentioned family conflicts stemming from publicly disclosing their homosexuality and their decision to transition. Consequently, poverty, abandonment, and discrimination were just some of the obstacles these women faced.

In our interviews with trans and travesti women, a constant point of focus was the violence and discrimination suffered at the hands of the dictatorship's police forces. In fact, many remembered the "law of morality and good behavior," specifically, as its legal justification. In some cases, simply being a trans woman sufficed. An anonymous trans woman, whom we refer to as Anita, was born in 1956 and worked as a hairdresser in Calama at the time of our interview. She was chased by the Carabineros while walking in the street:

> I was born in Antofagasta. I was in Valparaiso for six months and got stuck there because of the coup, nobody could come or go. I went back to Antofa when everything opened back up; the terminal, the station, the airport. . . . During that time, everything was restricted; there was a curfew, society wasn't itself, people were stressed out, nobody knew what was happening, and well, it was a very complicated time. We didn't have the freedoms we have today.
>
> *Were you ever detained for breaking the law of decency?* Yeah, a bunch of times, always for that notorious law of morality and good behavior. They grilled us for it. . . . I was a flashing neon sign, so easily noticeable, so when they wanted to justify their work they'd just catch whatever was easiest, and they'd take us and hold us there. . . .
>
> *Did they mistreat you in the police station?* Yeah, the treatment was ridiculous, mocking, putting you down, psychological. (Anita 2015)

These types of experiences were characterized by high levels of violence and a failure to understand what had happened. Invoking article 373 allowed for the detainment, repression, and intimidation of trans and travesti women without having to provide any rationale beyond an offense against morality and good behavior. Patricia of Santiago, born in 1959 and an ex-activist in the OTD, recounted an episode similar to Anita's:

> I think the hardest thing I went through was when they detained me for a decency offense. . . . It was for going around seducing men in the streets. I was seventeen years old, and they took me and they charged me with a decency offense. I wound up in jail. . . . I swear to God, up until this day I still haven't gotten an explanation as to why I was taken there. Being seventeen years old, being a minor, you'd think I should have been taken to a juvenile detention center, not jail. . . . They put me in a cell . . . and everything happened there, beatings, sexual abuse, and then they left me alone, naked. (Cinfuentes 2014)

Just like Anita, Patricia was not a sex worker and did not associate much with other trans or travesti women. The simple act of walking in the streets at night was enough to associate her with prostitution and "going around seducing men." In a time when human rights in Chile were violated every day, and given that there were no groups or spaces to denounce such abuses, trans and travesti women were severely underprotected in the face of police violence. In the case of travesti women working as prostitutes, repression was much worse. As Yokonda Montero, historic and important leader of Chile's first travesti organization, the Nefertiti group in Iquique, remembered:

> Damn, so much violence. They arrested us. A bus would show up, looking [for us] as though we were terrorists. There was a bus that would appear and there we were, women, men, and they said "giiiiiiirls" and we would run inside and they kicked down the door. They took us down from the roof, with machine guns and everything. I said, "But we're not terrorists, we're sex workers!" But off we went to the police station . . . where we arrived at six in the morning. They released the women, and we went to the prison, and they cut off our hair. We arrived as women, and they said, "Now, you gotta change out of those clothes you effing faggot and go to court." There were some women who were doing time, and they gave us five days. . . . They said it was for offenses to decency, because it was in the public street, and they cut our hair and we had to go and buy wigs, which they burned. They mistreated us. (Montero 2015)

Similar situations occurred in other places like Rancagua. Victoria, a hairdresser born in 1967, turned to sex work in the 1980s due to the impossibility of finding work as a trans woman. For Victoria, the dictatorship was one of the most difficult times of her life because of the abuses she experienced from police authorities:

> Yeah, in every way. I lived through the dictatorship, which was "heavy." Back then, offenses against morality and good behavior were still a thing. They'd catch you in the street dressed as a woman and they'd beat the shit out of you. They'd take you to a police station, fuck you up. You had to perform oral sex on all of the cops. They'd mock you. And you were in there for five days, without a fine, for offending morality and good behavior, offending decency and good behavior. (Yáñez 2014)

All of these crimes were allowed under the "moral authority" of the police forces, and there was no public knowledge of the mistreatment of trans and travesti women. *Cuerpos para odiar* (*Bodies to Hate*), the fanzine written by trans activist Claudia Rodríguez, also captures the experience of travesti women during the military dictatorship. Rodríguez refers to her writings as "travesti poetry," that is, poetry that tells of the violence, survival, and exclusion that travesti women experience in Chile. She tells of times when "we were huddled up treacherously like trash in an alleyway, cowering among ants away from the bangs of gunshots," alluding to brothel raids that resulted in the arrests, beatings, and disappearances of travesti women (Rodríguez 2014: 68).[6]

For trans and travesti women, one way to avoid such violence was to live in hiding, many times in the streets, due to the level of uncertainty and danger they faced. In this sense, the women interviewed could be considered survivors of Chile's military dictatorship, since many gay, lesbian, and trans people were tortured and murdered in brothels and shanty towns, acts for which no official documentation exists (Robles 2008: 17–18). Moreover, the democratic transition of the 1990s did not significantly change the situation of trans and travesti women. To the contrary, many of the women experienced the same violence after the military dictatorship ended, but it was now coming directly from the public (Garrido 2016: 21). In fact, the 1990s were characterized by social and regulatory conditions that prohibited the support of people whose sexual orientation and/or gender identity did not align with heterosexuality and gender norms (Miles 2015: 446). With the founding of the trans organization OTD in 2005, a space was created where Lorena, Victoria, and Patricia could begin to share and discuss their experiences of the dictatorship, forming the first collective memories of antitrans state terrorism in Chile and helping provide a preliminary diagnosis of historical and current violence against trans people in the country. Although too young to have lived through this type of repression directly, Kary Chamorro—thirty-two years old, from Talca, a member of Transgéneras por el Cambio (Transgender Women for Change)—told us of what she had learned from other trans women:

> I found out from my friends who, sadly, are no longer with us . . . that they pulled off their nails with pliers, they shaved their heads, they threw them around. There was a police station here, the Abate Molina in Talca. They carried out the operations at night. They detained all the women and took them all away in vans, the girls trying to escape on the roofs of the houses. . . . Like I was telling you, a lot of what we had was lost in the earthquake and when . . . Maribel died. She had a *casa de ambiente* (brothel) back then called the Jaula de las Locas.[7] Understand? And she had thirty or forty trans people in there, but the girls were inside the house. The Carabineros didn't let them come out into the street or even stop on the corner. They even extorted her, because every day the Carabineros would come by wanting three or four roast chickens and bottles of pisco. (Chamorro 2014)

As Kary signals, survivors of antitrans state terrorism have passed away over the years, dying from the physical and psychological effects of the dictatorship, poverty, drug and alcohol addiction, and the HIV/AIDS epidemic that wiped out a generation of gay men and trans and travesti women in Chile in the late 1980s and early 1990s. For example, in Patricia's case, being detained and beaten by the Carabineros in the 1980s resulted in the loss of three teeth and difficulties eating that persist to this day, not to mention psychological damage and a continued inability to comprehend the aggression and violence experienced. "I wanted to disappear," she said. Another case is Lorena, who told us that one of the major consequences of the violence she experienced during the military dictatorship was developing problems with alcohol and drugs, both of which continue to affect her health today:

> Look, I arrived at OTD because I came through the Community Mental Health Center, since that was where drug addicts and alcoholics went. Turns out I was in pretty bad shape, because I overdosed on crack and I was drowning myself in alcohol. I went to the hospital, and I said, I already had my apartment, and I was high as a kite from smoking crack there. I ended up falling asleep in some trashy place. I was hospitalized, and nobody came to visit me, nobody brought me a teacup, a towel, [not even] a roll of toilet paper. (López 2014)

In Patricia's story, just like the other testimonies, a sense of loneliness lingers as a result of family rejection (during and after the dictatorship), social, educational, and laboral exclusion, and of course, the violence suffered in the 1970s and 1980s. The lack of reparative policies for trans people further exacerbates the situation of these women, given that they tend to experience economic hardship while having to seek medical care, psychological help, dental work, and even treatment for chronic diseases. Moreover, the lack of official records and/or recognition of the LGBTQI people murdered, disappeared, and/or abused during the military dictatorship precludes the possibility of gaining true insight into the magnitude of such hate crimes in the 1970s and 1980s, particularly in terms of trans and travesti women. Rodríguez (2014: 78) alludes to stories that are told in the community about mass killings and crimes against trans women: "There's talk in the community that some of the bodies found in the mass graves in the north of our country, in the desert, were riddled with gunshot wounds. They were men's bodies dressed in women's clothes, show clothes, victims of the military period who had clearly been executed. And I wonder, 'How did they live and how did they die?'"[8] Despite the lack of official recognition of state terrorism against LGBTQI people in Chile, a small group of trans people tried to bring attention to the issue in the late 2000s. In 2009, President Michelle Bachelet created the Comisión Asesora Presidencial para la Calificación de Detenidos Desaparecidos, Ejecutados Políticos y Víctimas de Prisión, Política y Tortura (Presidential Advisory Commission for the Classification of Disappeared Detainees, Victims of Political Executions, and Victims of Imprisonment and Torture), commonly referred to as the Second Valech Commission (or Valech II). The purpose of the initiative was to make up for the shortcomings of the *Rettig Report* (Comisión Nacional de Verdad y Reconciliación 1991) and the *Valech Report* (Comisión Nacional sobre Prisión Política y Tortura 2004) by recognizing more victims of the Chilean military dictatorship. Some activists saw this as an opportunity to obtain legal recognition of the homo-, lesbo-, and transphobic violence of the dictatorial period. Patricia and Victoria, who met through OTD, tried to present their testimonies. Victoria explained: "I, along with a friend, filed a report when the Valech II opened, and we participated to see what would happen. . . . I was discriminated against. They hit me. I was sexually assaulted, not just for political reasons, but because of my sexual orientation and gender identity" (Yáñez 2014). For Victoria, the goal was to repay a historical debt owed to her friends and to the trans and travesti women that were killed between 1973 and 1990 at the hands of the police forces. Victoria, Patricia, and other OTD ex-activists of the same generation organized themselves to denounce the crimes and participate in the Valech II Commission. With the help of a lawyer, they began the process of having their testimonies included in the new report, but the lack of witnesses quickly derailed their momentum. According to the commission, their claims did not meet the requirements for consideration. Patricia explained, "We don't have witnesses, but what witnesses are you supposed to have? You could have been raped, there could have been blood, anything. You went through it. I know where they did those things to me. But witnesses? Where are they?" Victoria and Patricia agree that their attempt failed not just because of the commission's disinterest in including LGBTQI victims in the report but also due to the limited resources, tools, and legal support available to OTD.[9]

The cases of Patricia and Victoria form part of the 70 percent of cases not recognized in the Valech II Commission's report for failing to meet legal requirements, such as not proving political motivation, a lack of evidence, or not meeting the deadlines (*La Tercera* 2011). Both the Valech II and the commissions that preceded it reflect a patriarchal and heteronormative official discourse on human rights. The fact that even cisgender women were excluded from these accounts (Hiner 2009) demonstrates the difficulties these reports have incorporating issues around gender and sexuality. In the 2000s, several LGBTQI groups began to (re)appropriate discourses on, and expand the concept of, human rights to include LGBTQI subjectivities, fighting for antidiscrimination laws, marriage equality, and a gender identity law (Hiner and Garrido 2017). A key year in the recognition of LGBTQI people as "rightful subjects" was 2012, which marked both passing of the aforementioned Zamudio Law and the Inter-American Court of Human Rights' decision in the Atala case, which instructed the Chilean state to formally compensate Karen Atala for allowing the courts to take away her children on the grounds of her being a lesbian. Atala's was the first discrimination case on sexual orientation sent to that court and has become central in Latin American debates about sexual diversity and traditional family structures (Beltrán y Puga 2011: 217–18). Nevertheless, homo-, lesbo-, and transphobic violence during the civic-military dictatorship remains unrecognized, and the understanding of the concept of violence in the context of recent history in Chile continues to be limited. As activist Nicole Olmos of the Agrupación Arcoiris (Rainbow Group) in Antofagasta said: "These days, with the changes made by the democratic government, the wives of the detained and disappeared, their mothers, they all have access to free health care and to psychologists covered by the state. That's all well and good for the people that suffered, but who's speaking up for our *compañeras* who were killed for being homosexuals?" (Olmos 2015).

Final Reflections

To conclude, we would like to reflect on human rights, recent history, and trans history in Chile. Several areas remain understudied within Chilean historiography of the dictatorship. This includes the trans and travesti women who experienced violence during the dictatorship, not for political (partisan) reasons but, rather, because of the internal transphobia of police forces backed by article 373 and institutionalized discrimination. Though gender violence and sexual violence have been afforded more attention in recent years, little is known about the situation of LGBTQI groups during the Chilean dictatorship. Thus, the collective actions of and networks created between such organizations as Traves Chile (Santiago), the Amanda Jofré trans workers' union (Santiago), Arcoiris (Antofagasta), Nefertiti (Iquique), and OTD (Santiago, Rancagua, and Concepción) remain of utmost importance. These groups have been vital to the denouncement of transphobia and antitrans state terrorism, as well as to the creation of safe spaces for conversation and mutual recognition between trans and travesti people.

Nevertheless, the violence against LGBTQI people, especially antitrans state terrorism, must continue to be explored from a historical perspective. There also exists a related need to encourage more historians that identify as trans, travesti, queer, and more to complete programs of study in history—at both undergraduate and graduate levels—and to research areas of trans history. Currently, few trans people are studying or have studied in history programs, and even fewer trans academics are working in history departments at Chilean universities. We believe this must change as soon as possible so that a new field specific to trans, queer, gay, and/or lesbian studies can be considered and new lines of research opened.

In this article, we have explored the memories and oral histories of trans and travesti women who survived antitrans state terrorism in the 1970s and 1980s in Chile. These memories are characterized by raw, violent accounts of the military dictatorship, most of which indicate that the democratic transition did not significantly impact the rights of these women. On the contrary, article 373 remained in effect after the dictatorship. This explains why, within the discourse of human rights that emerged in the 1990s, the idea of violence was specifically focused on political violence and did not consider or problematize other variables such as gender, sexuality, ethnicity, and/or race until the 2000s. These trans and travesti histories are vital to the understanding of recent Chilean history from different perspectives that contribute both to historiography and to memory studies on state terrorism.

The physical and psychological effects of violence experienced during the dictatorship hinder the incorporation of trans and travesti women into Chilean society today, a situation further complicated by the absence of reparative policies. In this sense, healing for LGBTQI people is multifaceted, requiring recognition of both antitrans state terrorism and the historical violence they have suffered in Chile. Our interviewees demand diverse forms of reparation, but to produce such policies it is first necessary to understand the complexity of antitrans violence. This includes recognizing the effects of homo-, lesbo-, and transphobia and hegemonic heteronormativity, as well as acknowledging that this violence intersects with racism, sexism, economic discrimination, and prejudices related to idealized forms of corporality (Cornejo 2014: 274). Such policies would, ideally, entail a much larger debate within the areas of human rights and memory politics.

Hillary Hiner, a feminist historian with a PhD in history from the University of Chile, is assistant professor at the Escuela de Historia of the Universidad Diego Portales. Her research includes topics on genders, sexualities, feminisms, violence, oral history, and memory in the context of the recent history of Chile and Latin America.

Juan Carlos Garrido is PhD student in Latin American Studies at the Universidad de Chile and holds a master's degree in Latin American history from Universidad Diego Portales. His interests are the history of the LGBTQ movement in Chile and the construction of nation states in the Southern Cone.

Acknowledgments

The research that contributed to this article was carried out between 2013 and 2017 and funded by Fondecyt de Inicio project 11130088, "Una historia inconclusa: Violencia de género y políticas públicas en Chile, 1990–2010" (Hillary Hiner, researcher).

Notes

1. As we were reminded throughout our interviews, there are many other ways to refer to trans people. Older trans women often self-identified as *transsexuals*, *travestis*, *travas*,

locas, or *transfeminine*, while more recent terms included *marica/marika, queer/kuir/cuir, trans*, and even *nonbinary* or *gender fluid*. In the interest of simplification, we use *trans and travesti women*, in accordance with the most commonly seen terms n both Latin American academia and the vocabulary of trans and travesti activists. Furthermore, we found it important to include the term *travesti* because of the recent political demand that has arisen in Argentina by way of the Association for the Struggle for Travesti and Transsexual Identity, as well as in recognition of critiques of the term *trans* made by travesti activists, who consider it a "bougie" term that refers mostly to people of a higher social class. In this sense, the term *travesti* is associated with complex contexts often experienced by trans bodies, such as sex work and poverty.

2.   "Para las travestis, el Estado de Sitio es a diario. La rutinaria persecución policial, las acostumbradas restricciones a circular libremente por las calles portando una identidad subversiva, los permanentes obstáculos para acceder a derechos consagrados para todos/as los/as ciudadanos/as del país, entre otros, hacen de la vida travesti una vida en estado de sitio."

3.   To briefly explain how we came to employ this term: From the start, it was imperative that both authors recognize the specific violence experienced by LGBTQI people during the dictatorship as a form of state terrorism (concern seen, e.g., in (Hiner 2016, 2018; Garrido 2017). At the same time, we have also explored the violence that occurred after the dictatorship, engaging with the term coined by Doug Meyer (2008(, *antiqueer violence*, to emphasize its intersectional nature and the multiplicity of LGBTQI identities (see Hiner and Garrido 2017). Upon submitting this article, we had continued along this line, employing *antiqueer state terrorism* as a term that could cover more LGBTQI sub-jectivities that experienced state terrorism. The journal, however, preferred the term *antitrans state terrorism*, and the article does indeed focus solely on trans and travesti women. We thank coeditor Cole Rizki for the suggestion.

4.   These ellipses were added at the request of the journal, and we respect its position. We also recognize that any study about torture and violence entails a certain level of description of what happened. This is particularly important in instances when certain narratives have been systematically suppressed or erased and are in no way recognized by the state, as is the case with antitrans state terrorism.

5.   According to the research of Contardo (2012: 186–285), the Law on Antisocial Statuses enacted in 1954 during the Ibáñez del Campo government had the objective of cate-gorizing individuals who should be monitored and/or locked up for being potentially "toxic" to the nation. This included the homeless, drunks, drug addicts, and homosex-uals. Meanwhile, the Popular Unity government replicated the journalistic proclivities of the Cuban Revolution, publishing news that tied homosexuals to crimes of passion and perverse acts against minors.

6.   "Terminamos acurrucadas traicioneramente como basura en una callejuela cualquiera, acobardadas entre las hormigas por los estruendos de las balas."

7.   This travesti brothel is well known in more artistic circles, since celebrated photographer Paz Errázuriz took photos of the women there during the 1980s. For more information, see Donoso and Errázuriz 1990, which includes photo commentary and testimonies. The phrase "La Jaula de las Locas" refers to the French play *La Cage aux Folles* (this is the Spanish translation of the play's name in Chile). A US movie based on the play was translated as *The Bird Cage* (dir. Mike Nichols, 1996). Of course, there is also a play on words in the Chilean Spanish version, as *loca* is used to refer to effeminate gay men in

Chile, sometimes blurring into travesti women, as seen in much of Chilean author Pedro Lemebel's well-known work. For more on this topic see González 2014.

8. "Se cuenta en el ambiente que algunos de los cuerpos encontrados acribillados en fosas comunes del norte de nuestro país, en el desierto, eran cuerpos masculinos vestidos con ropas de mujer, de show, víctimas del periodo militar, con rastros de fusilamiento y me pregunto, ¿de cómo vivieron y cómo murieron?"

9. While opened during the first Bachelet government (2006–10), the Valech II Commission was mostly carried out during the center-right government of Piñera I (2010–14). The commission rejected more than 20,000 requests from people seeking to be recognized as victims of political imprisonment and torture. To this day, most cases have received no acknowledgment or explanation.

References

Arfuch, Leonor. 2013. *Memoria y autobiografía*. Buenos Aires: Fondo de Cultura Económica.

Beltrán y Puga, Alma. 2012. "Karen Atala vs la heteronormatividad: Reflexiones más allá de la discriminación por orientación sexual." *Debate Feminista*, no. 45: 217–45.

Berkins, Lohana. 2003. "Itinerario político del travestismo." In *Sexualidades migrantes: Género y transgénero*, edited by Diana Maffia, 143–55. Buenos Aires: Feminaria.

Butler, Judith. 2006. *Deshacer el género*. Barcelona: Paidós.

Comisión Nacional de Verdad y Reconciliación. 1996. *Informe de la Comisión Nacional de Verdad y Reconciliación sobre Violación a los Derechos Humanos en Chile 1973–1990 [Rettig Report]*. Santiago, Chile: Ministerio Secretaría General de Gobierno.

Comisión Nacional sobre Prisión Política y Tortura. 2005. *Informe de la Comisión Nacional de Prisión Política y Tortura [Valech Report]*. Santiago, Chile: Ministerio Secretaría General de Gobierno.

Contardo, Oscar. 2012. *Raro: Una historia gay de Chile*. Santiago, Chile: Planeta.

Cornejo, Giancarlo. 2014. "Las políticas reparativas del movimiento LGBT peruano: Narrativas de afectos queer." *Estudos Feministas* 22, no. 1: 257–75.

Dinges, John. 2004. *The Condor Years: How Pinochet and His Allies Brought Terrorism to Three Continents*. New York: New Press.

Donoso, Claudia, and Paz Errázuriz. 1990. *La manzana de Adán*. Santiago, Chile: Zona Editorial.

Feierstein, Daniel, ed. 2009. *Terrorismo de estado y genocidio en América Latina*. Buenos Aires: Prometeo.

Figari, Carlos. 2009. *Eróticas de la disidencia en América Latina: Brasil, siglos XVII al XX*. Buenos Aires: Centro de Integración, Comunicación, Cultura y Salud (CICCUS), Consejo Latinoamericano de Ciencias Sociales (CLACSO).

Figari, Carlos. 2010. "El movimiento LGBT en América Latina: Institucionalizaciones oblicuas." In *Movilizaciones, protestas e identidades políticas en la Argentina del bicentenario*, edited by Astor Massetti, Ernesto Villanueva, and Marcelo Gómez, 225–40. Buenos Aires: Nueva Trilce.

Garrido, Juan Carlos. 2016. "Historias de un pasado cercano: Memoria colectiva, discursos y violencia homo-lesbo-transfóbica en la dictadura militar y transición democrática en Chile." *Documento de Trabajo Instituto de Ciencias Sociales (ICSO)*, no. 24: 1–26.

Garrido, Juan Carlos. 2017. "Historias sobre un rosa amanecer: El movimiento homosexual y la transición democrática en Chile, 1990–2000." *Historia en movimiento: Acción política desde abajo*, no. 4: 94–107.

González, Melissa M. 2014. "La Loca." *TSQ* 1, nos. 1–2: 123–25.

Green, James. 1999. *Beyond Carnival: Male Homosexuality in Twentieth-Century Brazil*. Chicago: University of Chicago Press.

Green, James. 2012. "'Who Is the Macho Who Wants to Kill Me?' Male Homosexuality, Revolutionary Masculinity, and the Brazilian Armed Struggle of the 1960s and 1970s." *Hispanic American History Review* 92, no. 3: 437–69.

Hiner, Hillary. 2009. "Voces soterradas, violencias ignoradas: Discurso, violencia política y género en los Informes Rettig y Valech." *Latin American Research Review* 44, no. 3: 50–74.

Hiner, Hillary. 2016. "Mujeres resistentes, memorias disidentes: Ex presas políticas, militancia e historia reciente en Chile." *Conversaciones del Cono Sur* 2, no. 2: 4–8. conosurconversaciones .files.wordpress.com/2016/10/conversaciones-del-conosur-2-2-hiner.pdf.

Hiner, Hillary. 2018. "Putting the Archive in Movement: Testimonies, Feminism, and Female Torture Survivors in Chile." In *Beyond Women's Words: Feminisms and the Practice of Oral History in the Twenty-First Century*, edited by Katrina Srigley, Stacey Zembrzycki, and Franca Iacovetta, 204–16. New York: Routledge.

Hiner, Hillary, and Juan Carlos Garrido. 2017. "'Porque ser pobre y maricón es peor': La violencia anti-queer en Chile, 2000–2012." In *Malestar social y desigualdades en Chile*, edited by María Antonieta Vera, 195–223. Santiago, Chile: Ediciones Universidad Alberto Hurtado.

Hopman, Jan. 2000. "La sodomía en la historia de la moral eclesial." In *Masculinidad/es. Identidad, sexualidad y familia: Primer encuentro de estudios de masculinidad*, edited by José Olavarría and Rodrigo Parrini, 113–22. Santiago, Chile: Facultad Latinoamericana de Ciencias Sociales (FLACSO)–Chile/Universidad Academia de Humanismo Cristiano/ Red de Masculinidad.

Insausti, Santiago Joaquín. 2015. "Los cuatrocientos homosexuales desaparecidos: Memorias de la represión estatal a las sexualidades disidentes en Argentina." In *Deseo y represión: Sexualidad, género y estado en la historia reciente Argentina*, edited by Debora D'Antonio, 63–82. Buenos Aires: Ediciones Imago Mundi.

Jelin, Elizabeth. 2001. *Los trabajos de la memoria*. Mexico City: Siglo XXI.

La Tercera. 2011. "Mandatario recibió en La Moneda el segundo informa de la Comisión Valech." August 18. www.latercera.com/noticia/mandatario-recibio-en-la-moneda-el-segundo -informe-de-la-comision-valech/

Meyer, Doug. 2008. "Interpreting and Experiencing Anti-Trans Violence: Race, Class, and Gender Differences among LGBT Hate Crime Victims." *Race, Gender, and Class* 15, nos. 3–4: 262–82.

Miles, Penny. 2015. "Brokering Sexual Orientation and Gender Identity: Chilean Lawyers and Public Interest Litigation Strategies." *Bulletin of Latin American Research* 34, no. 4: 435–50.

Mott, Luiz Roberto. 1996. *Epidemic of Hate: Violations of the Human Rights of Gay Men, Lesbians, and Transvestites in Brazil*. San Francisco: Grupo Gay da Bahia/International Gay and Lesbian Human Rights Commission.

Radi, Blas, and Alejandra Sardpa-Chandiramani. 2016. "Travesticidio/transfemicidio: Coordenadas para pensar los crímenes de travestis y mujeres trans en Argentina." *Boletín del Observatorio de Género*. www.aacademica.org/blas.radi/14.pdf.

Robles, Víctor Hugo. 2008. *Bandera hueca: Historia del movimiento homosexual de Chile*. Santiago, Chile: Universidad de Artes y Ciencias Sociales (ARCIS)/Cuarto Propio.

Rodríguez, Claudia. 2014. *Cuerpos para odiar. Las travestis sobre nuestras muertes no sabemos escribir*. Santiago, Chile: Self-published fanzine.

Srigley, Katrina, Stacey Zembrzycki, and Franca Iacovetta. 2018. *Beyond Women's Words: Feminisms and the Practice of Oral History in the Twenty-First Century*. New York: Routledge.

Interviews

Anita. 2015. Interviewed by Hillary, Calama, Chile, August 23.

Chamorro, Kary. 2014. Interviewed by Hillary, Talca, Chile, July 28.

Cinfuentes, Patricia. 2014. Interviewed by Juan Carlos, Santiago, Chile, November 30.

López, Lorena. 2014. Interviewed by Juan Carlos, Concepción, Chile, November 15.

Olmos, Nicole. 2015. Interviewed by Hillary, Antofagasta, Chile, August 18.

Montero, Yokonda. 2015. Interviewed by Hillary, Iquique, Chile, August 25.

Yáñez, Victoria. 2014. Interviewed by Juan Carlos, Rancagua, Chile, October 11.

Mais Viva!

Reassembling Transness, Blackness, and Feminism

DORA SILVA SANTANA

Abstract The author focuses on the concept of *mais viva*, a term in Brazilian Portuguese that can be roughly translated as "more alive, alert, savvy." She theorizes the concept of mais viva as an embodied knowledge of black and trans resistance, a kind of critical awareness necessary for building self-love and building communities, along the lines of bell hooks's work. This discussion is an outcome of the dialogic theorizing that took place in the author's conversations with black Brazilian *travesti* activist Selen Ravache and her engagements with the work of Brazilian black feminist Beatriz Nascimento. The author argues that Selen's story is an instantiation of trans feminist work that taps on the Afro-diasporic legacy of fugitivity as refusal to lose oneself, even when one's self constitutes transformation, movement. She connects that discussion of fugitivity in the Brazilian African diaspora with the debates on trans and black fugitive principles in the United States indexed in the work of Tourmaline, Miss Major, C. Riley Snorton, Saidiya Hartman, and James Ford III, to name a few. Foregrounding black trans experiences from the southern hemisphere in relationship to transnational debates on gender, race, class, sexuality, disability, and nationality, among others, as part of a contingent conglomeration of elements, using Susan Stryker, Paisley Currah, and Lisa Jean Moore's terms, an assemblage constitutes one of the possibilities to rearrange, reassemble the ways we understand, move within, and intersect black, trans, and feminist studies.
Keywords black trans fugitivity, travesti, transfeminism, black feminism, Brazilian African diaspora

In 2014, when I did a summer visit from the United States to Rio de Janeiro, in the southwest part of Brazil, my fieldwork merged with my search for community.[1] The main questions that have guided my transitioning work, which were also present in that diasporic movement, are: What shifts are needed within knowledge production to make intelligible the embodied theorizing and call for action of black and trans people transnationally? What can the embodied experiences of black *travestis*/trans women/transsexuals in Brazil tell us about the ways black bodies are imagined, gendered, sexualized, and racialized locally but also connected with a broader experience in the African diaspora? What are the strategies of resistance and care for ourselves and our communities in the face of the haunting and material presence of death?[2] How do we imagine possibilities of

TSQ: Transgender Studies Quarterly ∗ Volume 6, Number 2 ∗ May 2019 **210**
DOI 10.1215/23289252-7348496 © 2019 Duke University Press

livable lives, of freedom, well-being, and transformative change, as we resist death? To address these questions, I have been invested in the methodology I call *papo-de-mana*, roughly translated as "sista talk," that is, foregrounding conversations with and from, as well as putting in conversation with, black women's voices, be they trans or cis, through face-to-face and also digitally mediated interactions as a site of dialogic theorizing. I draw from the legacies of already everyday ongoing practices of caring for one another with intimate checking ins between black and trans sisters, such as a phone conversation started by "E aí, mana!" (Hey sis!), and from the black feminist critiques acknowledging that black people have always been theorizing through oral history, as Barbara Christian (1988) reminds us. I engage with the work of April Few-Demo, Dionne Stephens, and Marlo Rouse-Arnett's (2003), who have used the phrase *sister-to-sister talk* to describe dialogic qualitative methodologies of working with/as/for black women that take into account an ethics of care but also a critical perspective on the not-taken-for-granted insider status of the scholar writing the work. According to Few, Stephens, and Rouse-Arnett, this approach stems from the usual meaning of the term *sister-to-sister talk*: "Afrocentric slang to describe congenial conversation or positive relating in which life lessons might be shared between Black women" (205). I engage in/promote all these kinds of conversations to access/build with the multisited archive of black trans women knowledge in Brazil. The multisited archive of black trans women experiences is accessed and activated then by our embodied knowledge and the body of work that we make available by us through our praxis of self and collective healing, caring, networking, and fighting, in relation to what is produced about us. The body of work can mean, but is not limited to, the ways we care for ourselves and for our communities, our relation to our landscapes, the discourses we create, the artistic work we produce in different media, and the imaginaries and emotions that are precariously disembodied into language.

Within that research for those conversations, in 2014 I took part in a support group called Trans Revolução (Trans Revolution). The group was consisting of a range of trans people that identified locally as *travesti, transexual* (transsexual person), *mulher trans* (trans woman), *homem trans* (trans man), and *não binária/o* (nonbinary people) from the outskirts of Rio. As I have transitioned along imposed sexually gendered racialized geopolitical boundaries between the United States and Brazil diasporas, I have learned to approach trans and transitioning as a nonlinear, undirected, dislocated, and localized movement, as also argued by such thinkers as Adela Vazquez and Jaime Cortez (2004), C. Riley Snorton (2011), and Kai M. Green (2015). The experiences of *vivências insubordinadas* (unsubordinated living) (Evaristo 2007) by people embodying undirected movement along the outcomes of (un)gendered racialized (Spillers 1987) formations that characterize the afterlife of slavery (Hartman 2007) within the Brazilian diaspora is what I calling *Afro trans vivências*. Despite the fact that trans experiences in Brazil comprise a range of embodiments beyond the scope of this article, and there is very important work being done, for instance, on black Brazilian trans masculinities by black trans activists and writers such as Leonardo Peçanha (2018), my focus here is on black trans women *em movimento* (in movement). *Women in movement* references the discussion brought by Brazilian black feminist Sueli Carneiro (2003) in "Mulheres em movimento," which refers to the participation of black cis women within feminist social movements in Brazil. When she does not talk about black women's movement but instead black women *in* movement, she covers the meanings of how black women move, the movement within communities and organizations, and black women participating in different movements. Movement becomes then motion, action, and collective organization.

Tourmaline (2016), a trans activist and writer, says isolation is one of the *I*'s of oppression. In this sense, black trans people and trans people of color socializing, sharing our stories, coming together to care for one another is indeed a form of trans revolution. Expanding Emi Koyama's (2003) perspective on the Transfeminist Manifesto, what I call *trans feminism* here constitutes a movement of liberation against gendered racialized oppression, a movement that draws from the archive of trans, black, and feminist legacies of theory and action. Considering that approach, the space of Trans Revolution and the travesti and transsexual people's movements in Brazil is trans feminist work. Reassembling blackness and transness in order to question which genealogies we want to the field(s) of black/ trans/feminist studies aligns with Angela Davis's (2016: 104) emphasis on feminist methods of "thought and actions that urge us to think about things together that appear to be separate and to disaggregate things that naturally appear to belong together." Assembling is also a practice of what Susan Stryker, Paisley Currah, and Lisa Jean Moore (2008: 13) call trans-ing, assembling "gender into contingent structures of association with other attributes of bodily being, and that allows for their reassembly."

Travesti in Brazil is one of the instantiations that embodies that trans movement. *Travesti* does not correspond to the English *travesty*, which is related somewhat to a performance in drag. *Travesti* is an identification that indexes a political position of resistance by trans femme/feminine/women's bodies of, historically, mostly black and people of color from poor communities. In one of my conversations with Jovanna Baby,[3] a black travesti, one of the pioneers in trans organizing in Brazil, she said travestis started the movement in the country by fighting against the police brutality especially directed toward sex workers. That struggle is part of a transnational movement, including the United States, against the violation of our bodies.

There is a political distinction but also an overlap and at times inter-changeable naming among *travesti*, *transexual*, and *mulher trans* in the country. The term *travesti* has been attached to a history of exclusion that has become classed and racialized in Brazil. The names, and the pictures posted before 2016, you will see in overwhelming numbers on the Transgender Day of Remembrance website (tdor.info) are those of violently murdered travestis, poor, usually black trans people whose lack of resources precluded their access to the technologies that would make them comfortable with their embodiment and connected with themselves in that manner. There are those cases that not making use of such technologies is not out of lack of resources but out of a choice of embodying their transness, womanhood or femininity not focusing on that aspect.

Transexuais (transsexual women) and *mulher trans* have acquired a more recent visibility on the media for cases of women like the Brazilian top model Lea T. Some trans people even having access to resources and embodiments that would place them as transsexuals by some people in that scenario, affirm their travesti identity because of that history of resistance. This erasure of the self-identification travesti is what the Brazilian trans scholar Luma Nogueira de Andrade (2016) calls *mulheramento da travesti* (womaning the travesti). When I ask Andrade if what she says constitutes an opposition to womanhood, she says, "No, I mean we are not *that* kind of woman" (Andrade, pers. comm. September 10, 2016). Calling oneself travesti is not a total negation of themselves as women, as Don Kulick (1998) has affirmed. It is a negation of an imposed dominant expectation of womanhood that centers on people who are cisgender, hetero-normative, able-bodied, elitist, and white. Thus, if we want to decolonize trans studies, it is important to understand that the resistance of translating *travesti* to just "trans woman" in English without contextualizing it comes with the risk of erasure of that history of fight in that part of the trans and black diaspora that is indexed by that term. It is also an invitation to think in which extent we are talking about *trans*, *trans woman*, and *gender nonconforming*, for instance, which are grounded in a local and Anglophone context, as reference of universality and unquestioned translation. *Transfeministas negras* in Brazil such as Hailey Kaas (2016) and Jaqueline de Jesus and colleagues (2014) invite us to think of *trans-feminismo* not just as an import but as resignified theory, a creation of our own that takes into account those range of experiences. For this reason, I choose to keep this text trans-linguistic not only to turn the text as a space of transition itself but also to reassemble the exemplarily linguistic categories we use to think trans, travesti, blackness and negritude. It is a reminder that this is a work of constant precarious translation. This is the context I would like to preface the introduction of Selen.

A luta é nossa! Viva a vida! (It Is Our Fight! Live Life!): Fugitivity as Refusal

Selen Ravache is a black travesti activist and performer who currently lives in the Rocinha favela in Rio de Janeiro. I met Selen in the group Trans Revolução. Since then, in our conversations I have shared my journey navigating academia as a black trans woman in the United States, and she narrates the everyday adversities and her persistence in keeping her current job as janitor in a hospital. Sharing our *vivências* (living) does not imply erasing or equating the power relations that take place in the institutional spaces in our lives, but it does offer an exchange that is different from me simply asking Selen to tell me about her life. Most of the women I talk with are very interested in the lives of black and trans people within the US diaspora. Also, since I am aware of the possible outcomes of the consumption of black trans women's stories in academia, the last time I called her I checked again that she would be comfortable with me using her story and her name within academic settings and texts; she replied, "Claro! A luta é nossa!" (Sure! It is our fight!) (Ravache, pers. comm., January 19, 2018). I smiled as I heard the familiar power in her voice. She had said that her job as a janitor was a transition from sex work, but not as a salvation job, since she emphasized what sex work made possible, including buying the land where she lives now.[4] This was a shift to a job with legal guarantees such as a retirement plan and benefits. She told me her presence at that job is also a testimony of what trans people endure to be in formal labor conditions:

> They say no, I say yes! They test me all the time! They test your patience, your desire/your horniness, your professionalism. They misgender me all the time; there are men grabbing their crouch and flashing on me, inviting me to this little room in the hospital. Just dumb tests! I know it is a trap. I know once I get there they will beat me to death and say I was harassing them or get me fired with just cause. They want to make me quit, but I don't quit. . . . I won't shed a tear for this people.

I told her I am very interested in the strategies we, as trans and black people, use to not be broken at the end of the day after transphobic racist aggressions. "What do you do?" I asked. Selen took a deep breath: "Wow, nobody ever asked me that question. . . . I'm gonna tell you what I do." She paused. "Eu vivo a vida, Dora! Eu vivo a vida!" (I live life, Dora. I live life!) The sentence had a different sonic quality. It was fast paced, assertive, intense, intentional. And she added, "They say we don't make until thirty. I am in my forties. *Opa!* That's a victory right there!"

The deaths of trans and black people mobilize more action than our living, our *vivência*. In their work on trans necropolitics, C. Riley Snorton and Jin Haritaworn (2013) use Achille Mbembe's concept of the politics of investing in keeping some alive while letting others die. One of the examples they discuss to address "the good" of the afterlife of black trans women is the death of Tyra Hunter, who died in a car accident after being refused medical care. That story mobilized funding for LGBT organizations that do not have trans women within their team or that do not impact them directly. Despite the fact that it is fundamental to honor the dead by demanding justice, there is a risk that trans women, especially black trans women, are discussed only as a corpse. The questions that are never asked—What do you do as a living being? What do you do to heal?—are the untold and unwanted stories I am interested in. It is fugitivity embodied in a living of refusal. Saidiya Hartman and Stephen Best (2005: 3) state that fugitive justice comes from that space between hope and resignation, a "political interval in which all captives find themselves," and "in this interval we find the mutual imbrication of pragmatic political advance with a long history of failure." Drawing from the work of authors such as Hartman, James Ford III (2015: 110) defines fugitivity as "the artful escape of objectification," whether that happens "through racialized aesthetic framing, commodification, or liberal juridico-political discipline."

"Viva a vida!" (Live life!) is a call to keep that space of hope within us as we move forward but aware of the oppressive systems we move within. Even "*viva!*" (alive) is a liminal space within us that carries the instances we felt dead due to humiliations and instances when we became more alive because our communities helped us continue. The last time I talked to Selen, she told me she sued her company and looked for local trans organizations to help her go public with her case. She said the last straw was when her company forced her to the use men's bathroom. She narrated: "As I slowly walked into the bathroom, I could see the crowed who gathered to watch. I felt like being stabbed that day! Help! I felt dead. My sister and some people tell me to be careful since the supervisor may have connections with some gangs here, but I am not afraid to die. They already killed me once. But of course, I need to take care of myself and be alert, you know" (Ravache, pers. comm., January 19, 2018). *Mais viva!*, more alert, more alive, is that embodied knowledge developed within that liminal space of not forgetting the imbrications between experiences of violence and the ways we find joy and acknowledgment and support, even if that comes in a micro-intimate level. For Selen, it is not only inviting friends over, staying connected to trans activist collectives, but also clubbing, hooking up, educating herself on her rights, and not quitting her job. Those liminal spaces of unsubordinated living that constitute the body of unwanted disruptive stories are what I call *vivencias* in conversation with what Brazilian black feminist writer Conceição Evaristo (2007) calls *escrevivencia*, that is, unwanted narratives written in words, drawn on the ground, complemented by our gestures: writing life, writing as living, a writing-living body, braking silences, being seen.

My own theoretical definition of *mais viva* is imbricated with the knowledge developed as strategies to experience one's own self-making with more intensity, a sense of urgency, by persistently refusing imposed distorted images and expectations. It means being more alive in the sense that living does not constitute a taken-for-granted existence that has only self-awareness as evidence. Living is not just self-awareness; it is also a form of a Fanonian double consciousness (Fanon 1967), in this case, multiple consciousness of oneself, of the other, and of the other in relation to oneself and histories of collective consciousness, an anticipation of scenarios that inform possibilities of routes of escaping violence by caution and also by experiencing joy, pleasure, and meaningful connections. It means "being-alive-savvy," it is not just being alive but more alive; it is transitioning in the world by transcending, trans-ing life. Being mais viva becomes the outcome and a condition to resist death. It is related to what bell hooks (2003a, 2003b) calls "vigilant awareness," the critical thinking needed to build community and build self love by challenging racist sexist and, I add, transphobic messages. Selen's story illustrates that refusal to quit, to accept the narrative of premature death as destiny, refusal to take in the expectations of failure, refusal to accept the imposed gendered and racialized ways of living, refusal of the shaming of her pleasure and her language by a politics of respectability.

Mais Viva! Fugitivity as *Quilombo*

To situate the discussions of fugitivity in the Brazilian black diaspora, here I introduce the work of Beatriz Nascimento, a black Brazilian historian whose work focuses on *quilombo* as a place of resistance. Related to Maroon communities within the Caribbean diaspora, *quilombo* can be the territories that have been occupied by descendents of fugitive slaves who settled their own communities and political systems. Quilombo can be a psychological place of resistance, which Nascimento calls her internal black (*negro interno*), the one that yells back inside when you're distraught and at times paralyzed by racism. Quilombo can be a place of joy and creative work that escapes from the imposed Eurocentric aesthetic and literary models to reconnect with Afro-diasporic rhythm and imaginary. Most black movements in Brazil mobilize blackness by remembering Zumbi, a black male figure who was a leader of quilombos of Palmares, during the beginning of the seventeenth century, famous for its resistance against the Portuguese Empire. What interests me in Nascimento's work is how she is trans-ing quilombo by narrating scenes in which black womanhood is tied to the refusal to accept that blackness needs to be imagined through a masculine figure and that womanhood needs to be imagined through a phenotype, or features associated to whiteness. In the documentary *Ori* (Gerber 2008), narrated by Nascimento, she says, "Zumbi, eu te vejo mulher" (Zumbi, I see a woman in you). What she means is that while Zumbi occupies a sign of black resistance in the Brazilian imaginary, the way of articulating the resistance of black women is to see a woman in/through and beyond the Zumbi representation of quilombo.

On her article "Acerca da consciencia racial" ("On Racial Consciousness"), Nascimento (2015a) narrates a scene of herself and another black girl called Jurema in their middle school, from whom she felt distinct but also related, given that Nascimento was submitted to similar humiliations. She says because she had short natural hair with tight curls, their classmates would say she was a boy and would laugh at her, with the complicity of the adults. In addition, Nascimento narrates, "one day, a child lifted my dress to see if I was a boy or a girl. That was the worst humiliation!" The other black girl, Jurema, went through what Andrade (2012) calls compulsory dropping out, which Andrade uses to address the experiences of travestis at school. I expand her concept to define it as mechanisms of gendered and racial violence that push nonconforming bodies out of school. Nascimento persisted despite the aggressions. She wrote that later in life she met that girl, and after sharing she was still in school, Jurema told her: "Don't let them do to you what they did to me!" Nascimento answered her call by dedicating her work to understand, remember, and share black women's legacies of resistance. As Nascimento is unable to talk directly to her at this point, Jurema becomes metonym for sister, and Nascimento (2015a: 110) addresses her by saying: "Jurema, how many things have not been taught to us. But I learned. I do not know if it was because I continued. . . . The Prejudice is the same, although today *sou mais viva!*" (I am more alive/savvy), and "do not let it destroy me as it has destroyed part of you." Being mais viva! is that healing knowledge that does not let you be in pieces; it is that knowledge that refuses losing ourselves by aggressions produced by racialized gendered violence that negates us. When Selen says "Viva a vida!" she joins the call by Jurema and Nascimento. I remember Selen told me that one of the things that motivated her to go public was not letting other girls develop urinary infections for containing themselves for being forced to go to men's bathrooms. It means "do not let them destroy you! *Seja mais viva!* Be more alive, savvy! Learn what they haven't taught us!," which is seeing ourselves. As we find in the work by Koyama and Miss Major, one of our elders who took part in the Stonewall riots, an important principle of trans feminism is the right for self-definition as self-care. Seeing our bodies, our knowledge production, creative work, and memories as places of resistance against racializing gendered violence against bodies that are not considered normative is where trans feminism and black feminism meet. In this sense fugitivity is a refusal of systems that keep us captive to situations that oppress us. For black and trans people, that refusal comes in the form of persisting in having a connection with ourselves and our communities. It is refusal to lose oneself.

Still Here! Refusing to Lose Yourself

Tourmaline (2016) reminds us that the Stonewall riots in New York were refusals of incarceration and police brutality as punishment for trans and queer people of color for connecting with our communities by just hanging out in a bar. The riots were also refusals of the criminalization of their gender-nonconforming embodiment that allowed them to connect with themselves. Tourmaline states that isolation is part of the logic of a carceral system that finds punishment as the solution for social issues. In "Making It Happen, Mama" Miss Major and Jayden Danahue (2015) say that the industrial prison complex is one of the most efficient systems to make you lose yourself: the criminalization of trans people, especially people of color; the gendering of the prison space by placing trans women in men's facilities; the placing of trans women in solitary confinement under the argument that is for their own protection. Miss Major created a pen pal program while she was a director of the Trans Gender Non-conforming and Intersex Justice Project. She narrates that the time when she was incarcerated for being trans, without receiving letters from the outside, she grabbed an stranger's postcard that said "hey girl" as a form of connecting and remembering who she was. "You can lose yourself in there," said Miss Major (308). Refusing to lose oneself is passing for ourselves to ourselves everyday in the face of misrecognition, it is the "agential power of affirming one's own reading of self" (Snorton 2009: 87).We turn passing from a narrative of dominant gaze on our bodies, as Sandy Stone discusses in the "Posttranssexual Manifesto" (1993), to a new meaning that keeps us sane, as an everyday affirmation of ourselves. For Selen, and for so many of us, refusing to lose her patience, her sanity, her professionalism, her job, her joy is the embodied everyday praxis of fugitivity. My goal here is not to present a prescriptive recipe of how to be alive. I am more interested in a kind of typology of archives of resistance where being mais viva constitutes a situated experience, that contingent movement that is trans and those routes of escapes that also defines blackness.

Thinking of black trans women experiences is not about replacing the sign that stands for blackness; it is about how we reassemble the ways we understand racialization of black bodies as gendered, with as many genders as we encounter, but at the same time that blackness also ungenders and is trans-ing bodies. Hortense Spillers (1987), whose work Snorton (2017) discusses, talks about the differences between bodies, which imply will and meaning to flesh, the zero meaning that is carved, beaten, unable to ward off violence and touch. When blackness becomes flesh, the kind of violence that goes across the board turns black bodies into ungendered flesh. The negation of black womanhood, for both cis and trans women, because our bodies are considered nonnormative, ungendered flesh, is not uncommon in the black diaspora. Lavern Cox takes the echoes of Sojourn Truth's voice in the text "Ain't I a Woman?" to address that kind of disavowal (Kerr 2013).

To do black trans feminist work is to bring in the fugitivity of blackness, that unspecified movement of transness and the gendered and ungendering racialization of bodies pointed out by black feminism. That work is also constituted by a vigilant awareness of self-critique, of being mais viva as we transition along our fields of study in order to unpack the silences and negations that we still find in those studies, especially when it comes to the experiences of black trans women. It is asking questions such this one posed by Davis (2013): "What would it be like to have, say, a black trans woman [like Miss Major] who has been involved in struggles against violence, struggles against the prison industrial complex? What would it be like for that woman to stand in as the sign of the category women?" What if we center black trans women like Selen Ravache within the discussion of trans feminist work by thinking of her persistence in being critically aware, mais viva!, and of taking care of herself as that knowledge of liberation? Davis's call invites us to think of the category "woman" as rhizomatic, as black trans women as hydrorhizomatic, along the lines of Édouard Glissant's work discussed by Treva Ellison, Kai Green, Matt Richardson, and C. Riley Snorton (2017): with floating roots, disturbed by the traces of the water's wake in the Middle Passage, as stated by Christina Sharpe (2016). I propose we think of womanhood by taking seriously the rhizomatic growth and visibility of black trans women's experiences and move away from the perspective that transphobic groups known as trans exclusionists and radical feminists have pushed. Their argument is that trans women are parasitic to womanhood. However, cutting us from the rhizomatic set of embodiments of *woman* does not push us to attach to other formations—it kills us. I interpret that seeing black trans women as the "the sign" does not mean putting us as sole representative of the category "women" alone; it doesn't mean the erasure of perspectives that takes black cis women, for instance, as a "sign" within black feminism—it pushes for the reconfiguration of the set of signs that we take to think womanhood. Requiring trans women and any other trans and gender-nonconforming person to prove our existence, to be asked for evidence of our existence, is what Sara Ahmed (2016) calls a hammering that chips away our being. Instead of hammering trans people, Ahmed proposes the hammering of the oppressive systems that keep us captive. She calls for an affinity of hammers, which is a collective work that understands the ways each of us is stopped along our journey. Affinity of hammers, she says, is an intentional work and an acquired ability to be attuned to the cases when someone is stopped. It is also being aware of when we are not stopped, which constitutes privilege. I have discussed here that intentional work of being tuned is already happening, but there is still a lot of work to be done. That kind of affinity of hammers reminds of what Audre Lorde (2014) calls choosing "the edge of each other's battles."

The other day I called Selen (pers. comm., January 19, 2018). Checking in on the phone is that kind of work that wins battles with intimate care for each other. As we talked, I expressed some of my concerns to honor these stories. Before I hung up, she raised her tone with excitement and said, "Vai lá mana! A luta é nossa! Viva a vida!" (You go sista! It is our fight! Live life!). I hung up. I let her energy sink in. And I told myself, *That* makes me more alive, mais viva!

Dora Silva Santana is as a black Brazilian trans woman warrior, scholar, activist, artist, and story teller of experiences embodied in language and flesh. She is an assistant professor of gender studies at John Jay College of Criminal Justice. She holds a PhD in African and African diaspora studies from the University of Texas at Austin.

Notes

1. I am from northeastern Brazil, so this trip provided a space of familiarity but was also a process of reconnecting since I had not lived in Rio before then.
2. I use *we, us, our, ourselves* as a political commitment of acknowledging my positionality also as a black Brazilian trans woman, despite the fact that I am critical of how my privileges such as access to academic spaces make me experience violence differently from most women I've worked with.
3. Jovanna Baby, phone interview by the author, May 20, 2016.
4. Selen Ravache, phone interview by the author, June 6, 2016.

References

Ahmed, Sarah. 2016. "An Affinity of Hammers." *TSQ* 3, nos. 1–2: 22–34.

Andrade, Luma de. 2012. "Travestis nas escolas: Assujeitamento e resistência a ordem normativa." PhD diss., Universidade Federal do Ceara, Brazil.

Andrade, Luma Nogueira de. 2016. "Travesti, Brazilian, and Professor." Paper presented at the Trans* Studies Conference, Tucson, AZ, September 10.

Carneiro, Sueli. 2003. "Mulheres em movimento." *Estudos Avançados* 17, no. 49: 117–33.

Christian, Barbara. 1988. "The Race for Theory." *Feminist Studies* 14, no. 1: 67–79.

Davis, Angela. 2013. "Feminism and Abolition: Theories and Practices for the Twenty-First Century." CSRPC Annual Public Lecture and CSGS Classics in Feminist Theory Series. YouTube, May 10. www.youtube.com/watch?v=IKb99K3AEaA.

Davis, Angela. 2016. *Freedom Is a Constant Struggle: Ferguson, Palestine, and the Foundations of a Movement.* Chicago: Haymarket.

Ellison, Treva, Kai Green, Richardson Matt, and C. Riley Snorton. 2017. "We Got Issues: Toward a Black Trans*/Studies." *TSQ* 4, no. 2: 162–69.

Evaristo, Conceição. 2007. "Da grafia-desenho de minha mãe: Um dos lugares de nascimento de minha escrita" ("On the Drawing-Graph of My Mother: One of the Birthplaces of My Writing"). In *Representações performáticas brasileiras: Teórias, práticas e suas interfaces* (*Brazilian Performatic Representations: Theory, Practice and Its Interfaces*), edited by Marcos Antônio Alexandre, 16–21. Belo Horizonte, Brazil: Mazza Edições.

Fanon, Frantz. 1967. *Black Skin, White Masks.* New York: Grove Press.

Few-Demo, April, Dionne Stephens, and Marlo Rouse-Arnett. 2003. "Sister-to-Sister Talk: Transcending Boundaries and Challenges in Qualitative Research with Black Women." *Family Relations* 52, no. 3: 205–15.

Ford, James Edward, III. 2015. "Close-Up: Fugitivity and the Filmic Imagination: Introduction." *Black Camera*, n.s., 7, no. 1: 110–114. www.jstor.org/stable/10.2979/blackcamera.7.1.110.

Gerber, Raquel, dir. 2008. *Ori.* Narrated by Beatriz Nascimento. Angra Filmes, DVD. www.facebook.com/uniaodetodasasnacoes/videos/documentário-or%C3%AD-beatriz-nascimento/1878768139068550/.

Green, Kai M. 2015. "The Essential I/Eye in We: A Black Transfeminist Approach to Ethnographic Film." *Black Camera*, n.s., 6, no. 2: 187–200.

Hartman, Saidiya. 2007. *Lose Your Mother: A Journey Along the Atlantic Slave Route.* New York: Farrar, Straus, and Giroux.

Hartman, Saidiya, and Stephen Best. 2005. "Fugitive Justice." *Representations* 92, no. 1: 1–15. doi.org/10.1525/rep.2005.92.1.1.

hooks, bell. 2003a. *Rock My Soul: Black People and Self-Esteem.* New York: Washington Square Press.

hooks, bell. 2003b. *Teaching Community: A Pedagogy of Hope.* New York: Routledge.

Jesus, Jaqueline Gomes de, Juliana Perucchi André Lucas Guerreiro Oliveira, Conceição Nogueira, Fábio Henrique Lopes, Felipe Moreira, Guilherme Gomes Ferreira, Liliana Rodrigues, Márcio Sales Saraiva, Natália Silveira de Carvalho, Nuno Santos Carneiro, and Viviane Vergueiro. 2014. *Transfeminismo: Teorias e práticas* (*Transfeminism: Theories and Practices*). Rio de Janeiro: Metanoia.

Kaas, Hailey. 2016. "Birth of Transfeminism in Brazil: Between Alliances and Backlashes." *TSQ* 3, nos. 1–2: 146–49.

Kerr, Ted. 2013. "Ain't I a Woman—Asks Laverne Cox, Actress, Producer, and Transgender Advocate." *Visual AIDS* (blog), April 19. Archived at www.scribd.com/document/350094470/Laverne-Cox-Ain-t-i-a-Woman.

Koyama, Emi. 2003. "The Transfeminist Manifesto." In *Catching a Wave: Reclaiming Feminism for the 21st Century*, edited by Rory Dicker and Alison Piepmeier, 244–59. Boston: Northeastern University Press.

Kulick, Don. 1998. *"Travesti": Sex, Gender, and Culture among Brazilian Transgendered Prostitutes.* Chicago: University of Chicago Press.

Lorde, Audre. 2014. "Performance of a Poem." In *The Edge of Each Others Battles: The Vision of Audre Lorde* [trailer]. YouTube, August 3. www.youtube.com/watch?v=zRntvB28CXI.

Major, Miss, and Jayden Danahue. 2015. "Making It Happen, Mama: A Conversation with Miss Major." In *Captive Genders: Trans Embodiment and the Prison Industrial Complex*, edited by Eric A. Stanley and Nat Smith, 301–13. Chico, CA: AK Press.

Nascimento, Beatriz. 2015a. "Acerca da cosciencia racial." In *Todas [as] diastancias: Poemas, aforismos e saios de Beatriz Nascimento*, edited by Alex Ratts and Bethania Gomes, 103–10. Salvador: Editora Ogum's Toques Negros.

Nascimento, Beatriz. 2015b. "Meu negro interno." In *Todas [as] diastancias: Poemas, aforismos e suios de Beatriz Nascimento*, edited by Alex Ratts and Bethania Gomes, 94–101. Salvador: Editora Ogum's Toques Negros.

Peçanha, Leonardo. 2018. "Visibilidade trans pra quem? Parte II—Um olhar transmasculino negro." *Negros blogueiros: Diálogos de nossa escrevivência* (blog), January 29. negrosblogueiros .com.br/leonardombpecanha/2018/visibilidade-trans-pra-quem-parte-ii-um-olhar -transmasculino-negro/.

Sharpe, Christina. 2016. *In the Wake: On Blackness and Being.* Durham, NC: Duke University Press.

Snorton, C. Riley. 2009. "'A New Hope': The Psychic Life of Passing." *Hypatia* 24, no. 3: 77–92.

Snorton, C. Riley. 2011. "Transfiguring Masculinities in Black Women's Studies." *Feminist Wire*, May 18. thefeministwire.com/2011/05/transfiguring-masculinities-in-black-womens -studies/.

Snorton, C. Riley. 2017. *Black on Both Sides: A Racial History of Trans Identity.* Minneapolis: University of Minnesota Press.

Snorton, C. Riley, and Jin Haritaworn. 2013. "Trans Necropolitics: A Transnational Reflection on Violence, Death, and the Trans of Color Afterlife." In *The Transgender Studies Reader 2*, edited by Susan Stryker and Aren Z. Aizura, 65 76. New York: Routledge.

Spillers, Hortense. 1987. "Mama's Baby, Papa's Maybe: An American Grammar." *Diacritics* 17, no. 2: 65–81.

Stone, Sandy. 1993. "The *Empire* Strikes Back: A Posttranssexual Manifesto." Austin: University of Texas at Austin, Department of Radio, Television, and Film. webs.ucm.es/info/rqtr /biblioteca/Transexualidad/trans%20manifesto.pdf.

Stryker, Susan, Paisley Currah, and Lisa Jean Moore. 2008. "Introduction: Trans-, Trans, or Transgender?" *WSQ* 36, nos. 3–4: 11–22.

Tourmaline [Reina Gossett]. 2016. "Making a Way Out of No Way." Keynote address at the Forty-First Scholar and Feminist Conference, "Sustainabilities." YouTube, March 7. www .youtube.com/watch?v=li6Y9nAwmf8.

Vazquez, Adela, and Jaime Cortez. 2004. *Sexile.* Los Angeles: Institute for Gay Men's Health.

The *Travesti* Critique of the Gender Identity Law in Argentina

MARTÍN DE MAURO RUCOVSKY

Translated by IAN RUSSELL

Abstract This article reviews the immediate *travesti* critique of the Argentine Gender Identity Law (law 26,743) in May 2012. Based on what was developed by Marlene Wayar, as an example of *sudaca* criticism and internal blasphemy, the *travesti* critique points out that the law does not recognize the specificity of the transvestite identity or its patent inequality, and it reintroduces the binary man/woman categories because it is capable of sanctioning only on the basis of a general population and within a liberal framework of state recognition. In this article the *travesti* critique of the Gender Identity Law is taken up to indicate a terrain of interrogations and challenges where the law becomes an instance of politicization, that is, where it becomes a field of strategic action and agency, but also a social tool and an instance of resistance, rejoinder, and reply.
Keywords Gender Identity Law in Argentina, trans interpretation, posthumanism, queer critique

In memory of Mayte Amaya, trans activist, piquetera, *and feminist from Córdoba, 1981–2017*

A fter Argentina's Gender Identity Law (law 26,743) was approved in May 2012, one particular reading gained special relevance regarding this legislation's significance amid the surrounding debate. On May 11, 2012, journalist and activist Marlene Wayar published the article "¿Qué pasó con la T?" ("What Happened to the T?"):

> The law has passed: congratulations to those who worked tirelessly toward this goal, special regards to those we brought together to reach it, and great thanks to those who accompanied in solidarity. Now, let's get to its real-life impact. This is a law for those who want to maintain the man-woman norm. And for those of

> us who had higher ambitions, it leaves us right where we were, or, better said, it relegates us to normalcy, into these solitary categories. (1)

Unenthusiastically, Wayar writes against the celebratory spirit of the law's passing and right to the heart of the activist camps. Wayar's article works to signal both the normative character and constrictive groupings of the man/woman categories. She highlights how the law holds up the erasure of a *travesti* identity. Exemplifying both *sudaca* criticism and a certain blasphemous quality,[1] the *travesti* critique calls attention to the fact that the law does not recognize the specificities of *travesti* identity or the blatant inequalities *travestis* face (especially considering the marked structural disparities, including the increased precarity and vulnerability faced by trans and sexually dissident collectives).[2] As well, a *travesti* critique demonstrates how the law reintroduces the man/woman binary, founded as it is on lawmaking for the general populace and within a liberal framework of state recognition.

This article takes on the *travesti* critique (Wayar 2012) of the Gender Identity Law (Ley de Identidad de Género, LIG) to illuminate, problematize, and challenge where the law becomes an instance for politicizing, which is to say, this article notes the sites where the law becomes both a form of strategic and agential action and a social tool of resistance and contestation. With our sights set on reclaiming an attentive, wholistic reading of the legal text, this article first probes the activist lineages behind the law's success that was conceived and promoted by and from trans activisms, their allies, and LGBTQI coalitions and therefore operates as a social and political toolbox rather than a mere legal instrument.[3] Second, the article analyzes, as a starting point, the group of fundamental displacements introduced by the law, which assumes that such legal tools suggest a pursuit of the construction and recognition of a "*popular* and subaltern subject" (Figari 2016: 235).[4] Further, these slippages wage an argument for expanding the limits of intelligibility of sexed bodies and identities. The series of displacements permitted by the law within the state also significantly challenge the functionality of the complex technological matrix of sexual difference (Butler 1990).

This article's third section considers this series of slippages and resignifications not only in a juridical, legal sense but also through the widening of the matrix of heterosexual intelligibility, the chain that ties sex, gender, and desire together. In this sense, the final section notes positions of intersection to illustrate spaces of alliance and political encounter. In other words, the LIG is a set of legislative tools with a definitive political power that both exceeds and sustains its own normativity. It is a toolbox associated with the dejudicialization, depathologization, decriminalization, and destigmatization of diverse trans bodies and subjectivities.

Contextualizing the Development and Debate

> To know what one will be is to live as dead.
> —Paul Nizan, *La conspiración*

The LIG arose from a process filled with debate and struggle by trans activists and their allies. The relatively recent nature of the struggle makes it easily traced through a series of predecessors in the 1990s to the organization and politicization of trans, *travesti*, and transsexual activisms. Some important groups to mention are Travestis United, Association of Argentine Travestis, Organization of Travestis and Transsexuals of Argentina (led by Nadia Echazú), and Association for the Fight for Travesti Transsexual Identity (led by Lohana Berkins). The legislative proposals and political agendas around the right to identity and advocating for integrated attention to health care began to take shape in the first decades of the 2000s. These years saw the consolidation and greater public visibility of activisms of sexual dissidence, along with the formation of the Anti-Discrimination Movement of Liberation (led by activist Diana Sacayán) in 2002; the Federación Argentina LGBT (FALGBT) in 2005; the National Front for the Gender Identity Law (Frente Nacional por la Ley de Identidad de Género, FNXLIG) in 2010; Trans Men of Argentina; and the Transgender Future organization; among so many others.

The LIG recognizes that the right to gender identity is a fundamental human right as stipulated by the Yogyakarta Principles[5]: "Gender identity is understood as the internal and individual way in which gender is perceived by persons, that can correspond or not to the gender assigned at birth, including the personal experience of the body. This can involve modifying bodily appearance or functions through pharmacological, surgical or other means, provided it is freely chosen" (LIG, article 2).[6] The right to gender identity, then, is directly linked to the modification of the body. Precisely for this reason, the right to identity cannot be separated from legal access to health care, "through pharmacological, surgical, or other means." Additionally, it is not by any means coincidental that the introduction of equal health rights within the LIG can be upheld through the right to identity's own normative forces. The granting of such rights is predicated on the concept of a human right to identity as inherent to the struggle of other human rights groups. Particularly, the Grandmothers and Mothers of the Plaza de Mayo facilitated a discourse on the "right to identity" by invoking it repeatedly with reference to the restitution of the infants and children taken during the final civic-military dictatorship (1976–83). The LIG came to resignify and displace the available social grammars around the social danger of *travestismo*, entrenched in hygienic, criminological, and legal discourses since the founding of the nation-state. Further, as a legacy of the second half of the twentieth century, the LIG displaced transsexuality as the dominant rhetoric. As Leticia Sabsay (2011) and Anahí Farji Neer (2017) suggest, state regulation looks on both *travestismo* and homosexuality as threats to the nation and has tried to eradicate them through a series of norms primarily instated through police edicts (introduced in the 1930s in Buenos Aires and the 1950s in other provinces) and, later, through misdemeanor codes (from the 1990s on).[7] Both types of legislation incentivized the penalizing, disciplining, and surveilling of illicit conduct, as well as the policing of public spaces (Sabsay 2011). These very codes and edicts guaranteed that criminalization and police persecution remained a constant in the daily lives of trans and *travesti* sex workers, who were subjected to raids, pogroms, *razzias*, forced disappearances, random jailing, and systematic harassment. Although not prohibited by or classified in the penal code, trans sex work simultaneously became a de facto criminal act (Berkins and Fernández 2005; Berkins 2008, 2015).

Additionally, medical practice inherited and passed along ideas from the likes of Harry Benjamin's endocrinological discourse, Norman Fisk's North American psychiatry, John Money's medicalizing discourse, and even more renowned diagnostic manuals and protocols, like the International Classification of Diseases and the *Diagnostic and Statistical Manual of Mental Disorders*, both of which still hold currency in Argentina's biomedical discourse today (Farji Neer and Cuenya 2014; Farji Neer 2017). From the mid-1950s, biomedical and psychiatric discourses made transsexuality an object of regulation by the parts of the legal and medical fields handled by the state. In Argentina, until the approval of the LIG, a standard did not exist to regulate access to trans rights. Rather contrarily, a group of guidelines did exist that judges would cite in deciding each particular case. The precedents invoked by magistrate judges before each case were either the Law of Exercise of Medicine or the laws of identification of persons (law 24,540) and name (law 18,248). These established the obligation "not to surgically intervene in order to modify the sex of the infirm, save that such intervention be effected after a judicial authorization." These laws also stipulated "the duty to identify the newly born and established that these data could only be modified provided just motive to intercede as expressed in a judicial resolution" (Farji Neer 2017: 76–77).

Facing each verdict, request, or process, the judicial system proceeded to investigate the sexuality of trans persons, under the double understanding of *travestismo* as social danger and transsexuality as reigning device and rhetoric. Persons who wished to modify their sexed body and/or alter their genitalia and reproductive organs had to undergo a lengthy process under express judicial authorization. Through these protocols, trans people were obliged to submit themselves to medical examinations. These included psychiatric, psychological, and internal and external physical tests based on the idea that sex as assigned at birth is natural. This rhetoric persisted in both medical evaluations and judicial readings of trans embodiments: "The idea of understanding the transsexual subject as someone trapped in the wrong body suggests that the criterion of hegemonic femininity and masculinity should remain unquestioned and uninterrupted" (Litardo 2013: 243). Under this notion, the proof of sex was reified as a tool. That is to say, the existence of a wrong body presupposes its opposite, a true sex and a correct body. For the state's institutions, then, genitality, psychological determinisms, and the natural equivalence between body and identity all served as foundations to colonize varied corporealities and reaffirm the universality of the cissexual norm.[8] For Argentina, such protocols produced sex as constitutive of the ontological ends of gender and sexed bodies.

Medical evaluation and diagnostics became as much a legal requisite to access sex and documentation changes as an exercise of de facto legal persecution. They expressed the very form of power relations in which some bodies are forced to take medical and judicial steps even to gain access to the acknowledgment of their rights. These discourses provided the model for the law to unfold its strategy for making the human easier to identify: "Pathologizing is the first requisite along with the fulfillment of a certain appearance of the body: (1) Such a person's body must resemble as closely as possible the body of the sex to which they decide to belong and (2) Additionally, such person must be irreversibly sterile" (Cabral 2012: 258–59). The indisputable premise that sustained such authorizations and court verdicts could trace its argument backward through a long tradition of clearly eugenic and punitive threads cross-stitched throughout Argentine dogma.[9] As such, the sterilized trans body represented the political promise of a collective temporality—a normative, shared future. The monsters shall not multiply.[10] By requiring sterilization, the population could be reassured against the presence of potential risk of contagion, reproduction, and further growth of the trans demographic. Health scares or biopolitical construction functioned as a eugenic or thanato-political mishap. In the name of a life to protect—in the name of the paradigmatic model, the child—violence was deployed for the continuity of the species, the citizenry, the people.

From Social Danger to Identity as Human Right

Between 2008 and 2012 the provinces of Buenos Aires, Santa Fe, Santa Cruz, Río Negro, Neuquén, Formosa, and Tierra Del Fuego abolished or partially modified the articles pertaining to their misdemeanor codes that penalized acts of "dressing with clothes or attire of the opposite sex, indecorous outfits, exhibitionism, or causing public scandal" (Tierra Del Fuego provincial law 77/59, sanctioned in the year 1959).

Another important milestone occurred with the recognition of the Association of Struggle for Travesti-Transsexual Identity as a legal body, a recognition the group had been demanding for four years until the Supreme Justice Court offered a favorable opinion in 2006. The Supreme Justice Court considered, in that period, that elevating the quality of life of a systematically vulnerable group would benefit the entire community (Fernández, D'Uva, and Viturro 2008–9). In 2010 the directive councils of several departments of different national universities (La Plata, Buenos Aires, Comahue, Rosario, and Tucumán) created internal guidelines guaranteeing the recognition of identities within their institutions. The National University of Córdoba even instantiated guaranteed health care access and corresponding medical treatment through its teaching hospital (De Mauro Rucovsky 2015: 25).

Additionally in 2010 — after the effective passing of gay marriage — two groups of trans and allied activists began to network and lobby with distinct political advocacy groups with their sights set on the passing of the LIG. From there, both the FALGBT and the FNXLIG brought forth judicial action in the form of protection orders and precautionary self-help measures. The groups strategized that the reading of judicial opinions and orders in their favor would secure jurisprudence and, consequently, advance the treatment of their bill. In any case, the activist groups procured judicial and legal measures that recognized sexual rights without required submission to medical or psychological examination and that sought to attend first and foremost to the autonomy of whomever demanded it.

The trans activism groups rallied around the FALGBT coalition and, in collaboration with the Spanish LGBT Federation, promoted two legal projects, including the filing of bills 7644-D-2010 and, with the help of FNXLIG, 8126-D-2010. The first version, bill 7644-D-2010, provoked a bit less controversy due to its mode of presentation. By separating the recognition of chosen name from that of access to medical care, the project created a hierarchy of the rights in play and, at the same time, an uneven reading between modes of embodiment and identification (Litardo 2015: 2). Ultimately, though, this first filing proved problematic because it demanded a stable, permanent gender identification and required the presentation of a legally certified declaration to claim the right to amend state documents. In one way or another, the sovereign role of the state presented itself as an administrative and surveilling apparatus of gender control, which dangerously mirrored Spanish state law 3/2007 with a similarly pathologizing and paternalist spirit.

For their part, trans and allied activisms united around the FNXLIG to draft a version of their own law (file 8126-D-2010, shared with the FALGBT), which served as the base for the ordered, definitive text of the LIG. The draft mostly concerned the amendment of identification documents and access to medical treatment in order to construct a bodily image corresponding to gender identity. Both points were included in the Compulsory Medical Plan and made free of charge. This version was based on the Yogyakarta Principles of international legislation around questions of sexual orientation and gender identity, especially the cited second article regarding the definition of gender identity. After a series of advocacy negotiations in situ, two proposed amendments were eliminated in the National Front's original project for the LIG: the second article referring to age limits "confirming the minimum age of sixteen years" and the ninth article on abusive therapies that forbid the genital mutilation of intersex persons: "It remains prohibited that intersexual children and adolescents be intervened surgically due to their intersexuality by the sole decision of a doctor, guardian or parents without taking into account the superior interest of the child or adolescent plainly and with their consent. Intersexuality does not constitute a pathology that needs be corrected clinically." As both activist groups came to an agreement and the Chamber of Deputies approved the bill in November 2011, the Gender Identity Law (no. 26,743) reached final approval in the Senate on May 9, 2012.

The LIG's legal and political standards mark a meaningful shift in the exercise of bodily autonomy ranging from administrative and judicial decision making on trans corporealities—that the civil servant on duty authorizes access to certain rights—to the autonomous power of decision on bodily modifications facilitated by the LIG. The sixth article of law 26,743 defines the procedures exactly as follows:

> The public officer will proceed—without any additional legal or administrative procedure required—to notify the amendment of the sex and the change of first name to the Civil Register . . . so it will issue a new birth certificate incorporating the said changes, and to issue a new national identity card reflecting the amended sex and the new first name as now recorded. Any reference to the current law in the amended birth certificate and in the new national identity document issued as a result of it is forbidden. The procedures for amending the records as described in the current law are free, personal and do not require the intervention of any agent or lawyer.

With the same tone, another of the LIG's substantive changes effectively dismantled the biomedical, pathologizing standard (classified according to such psychiatric protocols as "gender dysphoria") that forced trans persons to be sterilized to gain access to bodily and biotechnological modifications. From there, even within the normative basis of the LIG, it addresses "bodily and biotechnological modifications" as "a right of comprehensive health and, at the same time, are not to be an obligation." As such, the fourth article indicates the legal requirements:

All persons requesting that their recorded sex be amended and their first name and images changed invoking the current law, must comply with the following requirements:

1. To prove that they have reached the minimum age of eighteen (18) years
2. To submit to the National Bureau of Vital Statistics or their corresponding district offices, a request stating that they fall under the protection of the current law and requesting the amendment of their birth certificate in the records and a new national identity card, with the same number as the original one.
3. To provide the new first name with which they want to be registered.

In no case will it be needed to prove that a surgical procedure for total or partial genital reassignment, hormonal therapies, or any other psychological or medical treatment has taken place.

The law makes explicit that those same "surgical and hormonal procedures cannot be an obligatory requirement for the state as the price to recognize gender identity" (Cabral 2012: 1). As such, in human rights, the LIG is a politics of reparation that recognizes gender identity on two levels. First, following a mechanism of recognition, the national identity documents can be modified by new documents in which self-identified gender identity is validated, as pronounced in the above-cited sixth article: "The public officer will proceed—without any additional legal or administrative procedure required—to notify the amendment of the sex and the change of first name to the Civil Register." The amendment of sex as well as change of name and image can be obtained beginning with a personal step, an expression of one's own volition, at the offices of the Civil Register. No longer is it necessary to depend on judicial authorization, pathological certification, or a confirmation of will to receive surgical intervention. Likewise, such a right to be recognized also implies the amendment of other legal documents including a modified birth certificate.

Second, the law guarantees obligatory access to the medical system, as pronounced by the eleventh article: "Public health officials, be they from the state-, private- or trade union-run health insurance systems, must guarantee in an ongoing way the rights recognized by this law. All medical procedures contemplated in this article are included in the Compulsory Medical Plan." The LIG guarantees access to health rights within the Compulsory Medical Plan and grants, precisely due to it, that the Ministry of Health comply with hormonal treatments and sexual prostheses, transition processes, and correspondent surgeries for any person who may so desire. Each of these is covered by the three health subsystems (public, private, and trade union). Lastly, the LIG also includes migrants, in accordance with the legal requirements established by decree 1007/2012 (Farji Neer 2017: 110).

The Trans Experience between *Travesti* Cuts and Sutures

> Papers may say one thing,
> But nature says something else!
> They'll be man or woman until the end of their days.
> —Roberto Jacoby and Syd Krochmalny, *Diarios del odio*

It certainly did not take long for criticism of the LIG to arrive. One could even consider the critiques as a constitutive part of the process of planning and development within activist circles themselves. As indicated, for Wayar (2010: 1), *travesti* criticism was shaped from the beginning as an operation of intragroup blasphemy. *Travestis* do not fit the paradigm of citizenship because the only subjects who fit this category are men and women. Wayar adds that "we *travestis* are not men or women; we are constructions of personal substance, our own absolutely and highly personal body of laws" (1). Wayar's position is compelling because it indexes a problem in the very articulation of the legal standard set by the LIG. *Travesti* identity—a political identity that carries its own weight within South America's trans activisms—still lacks formal recognition within the LIG's reparational framework: "What is the problem with legitimizing the categories of man and woman? Because one identity remains ultimately canceled out: the *travesti* or the trans ceases to exist. What does this law demand of us? That we stop being that very thing that we are and that should be recognized as our identity" (Wayar 2012: 1). As well, the LIG's definition of gender identity requires truth and stability in the self-identification of the subject. This notion presupposes not only the subject's disjointed perception of the body but also a necessary correlation between self-perceived identity and the subject's very existence: "Every *compañerx* that changes their ID card will be un-inscribing themselves of a trans identity so that the state can read him or her as they identify them 'man' and 'woman.' And what happens if our *travesti* is still noticeable? It will be our fault for not making enough of an effort to appear as what we say we are" (Wayar 2012: 1). On this point the LIG does not permit the proliferation of identities, genders, and sexual positions because the state reads them and reduces them to the man/woman binary. It is worth signaling that, if the LIG demands subjects' very existence and stability through their own self-perception, this requirement is merely a bureaucratic detail. This administrative identification only requires an identification document. And even more, the LIG imposes neither a quota in the requests of document changes nor medical treatments or surgeries, meaning that a proliferation or disturbance of identities, genders, and positionings is still possible within the normative frame-work of the law.

However, Wayar emphasizes that the recognition of transness in both social terms and its legal articulations would possibly be settled by the majority of the population's measures on behalf of *all* citizens, but for no one in particular. Here, the chain of equivalencies tends to erase the specific, material nature of trans reality: whether of trans men (still the least visible in the vision of sexual dissidence and LGTBQI coalitions), *travestis*, transgendered people, or trans-sexuals. The political *travesti* identity, notably born out of the Río de la Plata area of South America, lacks specific recognition within the reparational mech-anism of the LIG. Additionally, as Wayar (2012) seems to note, the law's process of dispute and negotiation was hatched in the name of a markedly liberal trans model of citizenship, which is to say, it developed in terms of individual, pos-sessive, and personal rights. Although the same critique is highly valuable, the radical nature of *travesti* identity would also be inscribed in a liberal model of citizenship, even if the T were included within the LIG's standards.

Following this position, we should signal that, to paraphrase Carlos Figari (2012: 48), this discussion of *travesti* criticism should be necessarily analyzed through its usefulness and locally situated emergence, but not at the expense of the essential value of a critical perspective. This viewpoint is suggested by such recent reports as *La revolución de las mariposas* produced by the public trans-inclusive high school Mocha Celis in 2017, *Cumbia, copeteo y lágrimas: Informe nacional sobre la situación de las travestis, transexuales y transgéneros* by Berkins in 2007, and its predecessor *La gesta del nombre propio: Informe sobre la situación de la comunidad travesti en la Argentina* by Berkins and Josefina Fernández in 2005. The activist experience in the southern hemisphere—attached to deep inequality and social conflict—allows for the articulation of subaltern and popular subjects (Figari 2016: 235) and specific genealogies across boundaries.

As such, we would do well to consider another question: under what sociohistoric conditions and in what sense did trans activisms organize their agenda and develop the LIG and its demands? And, further, must the LIG encompass only the trans population? Or, should it perhaps recognize specifically political identities like *travesti*? Even when the identities in the LIG, and within the whole Argentine legal system, are recognized as a binary, the political and legal power of the text is indubitably located in exposing the malleability of categories like masculinity and femininity. They are inherently *not* like the epigraph from this section's beginning: "They'll be man or woman until the end of their days."[11] In this sense, the recognition in the LIG is not tied to specific identities—not trans-gender, *travesti*, or transmasculine—but rather accounts for the undecidability of gendered ways of living: "Gender identity is understood as the internal and individual way in which gender is perceived by persons, that can correspond or not to the gender assigned at birth, including the personal experience of the body. This can involve modifying bodily appearance or functions through pharmacological, surgical or other means, provided it is freely chosen. It also includes other expressions of gender such as dress, ways of speaking and gestures" (law 26,743, article 2, "Definition"). What is signaled by the law's articles, especially in the second article quoted above, is the definition of gender identity, taken in turn from the Yogyakarta Principles.

The recognition of gender identity in the LIG marks a minimum departure point—and not an arrival—with respect to the state of law, which is to say, it does not pronounce itself on the effective mechanisms to resist inequality of the trans population, but it achieves, as was signaled, the departure point that no citizen has more rights than another. This is the scale on which these activisms and the development of the LIG can be understood. No specific law can resolve the entirety of the trans agenda, but it does constitute an advance—always partial—in that direction. Several subsequent examples of this path have emerged in the wake of the LIG: Buenos Aires's provincial law 14,783 on trans labor quotas, named after Amancay Diana Sacayán and creating job posts for trans workers, the provincial laws following this on trans labor rights, the projected national law presented in Argentina's congress (bill S-4214/16), and the projected law No. 2526-D-2016 with the hashtag #reconocer es reparar (to recognize is to repair) on the "reparational rules for victims of institutional violence due to gender identity" (Cosecha Roja 2016).

In this sense, the passing of the LIG implies a transformation for the state in its relation to the manner in which it executes the legal and political recognition of trans identities and embodiments. But also, the LIG functions as a mechanism of expansion and disruption of identitarian recognition and its matrices. This reading of the law supposes a displacement, perhaps a critical method, within the juridical mechanism. Specifically, the law's productivity lies in its function as legal instrument and the LIG's potentiality to become not only content or focused theme but also a strategic field of action. Therefore, this law enables both a zone of political immanence and a critical reading of the matrix of cishetero intelligibility.

The LIG, as a legal, social, and cultural tool, not only allows for the amendment of the appearance or function of the body between biological sex and self-perceived gender—the recognition of self-perceived identity and corresponding medical access—but also permits document changes without either obligatory psychiatric-psychological treatments or bodily modifications and surgeries. As the fourth article indicates, it is important to recall: "In no case will it be needed to prove that a surgical procedure for total or partial genital reassignment, hormonal therapies, or any other psychological or medical treatment has taken place." In this final sense, a political potentiality dwells within the very legal letter of Argentina's identity law. In its very inner workings, it allows for different people to embody a particular gender and corresponding gendered name. As previously indicated, the political and legal potency of the text lies undoubtedly within its exposure of masculinity and femininity as modifiable categories. It speaks to a slippage of enormous political power where legal recognition of identity is not subordinated to corporeal biologization of identities (the ability to carry a legible, intelligible body according to biomedical parameters). As signaled in the seventh article, the law likewise will not subject trans people to psychiatric experts or biomedical exploration by committees: "In all cases, the number in the persons' national identity document will be relevant over the first name or morphological appearance of the persons, for identification purposes" (LIG, article 7). In this way, access to surgery and bodily modifications is not dependent on the named change, as indicated in the eleventh article: "There will be no need to prove the will to have a total or partial reassignment surgery in order to access comprehensive hormonal treatment. The only requirement will be, in both cases, informed consent by the individual concerned." It addresses, then, a twofold resignification: in gender-expressive naming and in terms of sexed embodiment.

Facing the LIG: "I Reclaim My Right to Monsterhood" — Susy Shock

The LIG implicates an advance in terms of human rights with respect to its legislative content. It refuses the subjection of trans bodies and subjectivities to courtrooms, pathologies, and criminalization. It also signifies the dismantling of a juridical matrix that exposed trans diversities to both eugenic and pathologizing forces. Even with these gains, the law still raises a series of questions. What are in play around the LIG's political borders are the norms of social recognizability of sexed subjectivity. In this same sense, the LIG's existence does not change the experience or social treatment of gender. However, the law's overarching spirit unleashes an understanding of the normative power forces that construct sexed bodies. Following the LIG, what political uses and sexual counterpractices are possible? As a social procedure and toolbox, what short circuits and destabilizing effects does the LIG permit and enable? The LIG effectively has the virtue of assuming identity in difference. From there, masculinity and femininity are malleable and modifiable categories and, as such, are political categories before ontologies. In line with this thinking, Blas Radi (2013: 3) states:

> What defines a man or a woman now? What gynecologist specializes in trans women? Is there a urinal designed for men with a vagina? If a trans man has relations with a cis man is he homosexual? And if he has relations with a cis-woman, is he heterosexual or vice versa? Or is he homosexual only if he is with

another trans man? To what degree is the act "homo" if one man has been operated and the other has not? Or, in accordance with the question proposed previously, before the law, does a pregnant trans man become a father or a mother?

These questions arise since, in order to be human, everyone needs a legible gender. Expressed differently, if the matrix of heterosexual intelligibility sustains itself on the apparent causality that links biological sex → gender identity → gender expression → sexual orientation or desire, then this law makes possible the disruption of this cisgender-heterosexual causal chain. As has been signaled, people could very well amend their name identification and retain their assigned biological sex. It is also possible within this mechanism to modify the assigned biological sex through the medical system without replacing the administrative and named documents.

In the preceding pages, *travesti* criticism was taken on from different dimensions. Beyond the tautological character of the criticism to signal the inevitable reproduction of the gender binary, the LIG effectively reifies the binary in the same way the entirety of the Argentine legal system does. Such a provision seems unquestionable. This reading, though, advocates for other sexual epistemologies that might avoid such reifications of the stale, stereotypical division between the LIG and the *travesti(s)*. Both against and through these epistemologies, what emerges is a politics of transversal and trans alliance that deontologizes sexual difference and the matrix of hetero-cis sexual intelligibility and opens new configurations of sexed bodies, subaltern and popular subjects, and their political strategies.[12]

Since the LIG's passing until now, we have observed the expansion of the LIG in its social, strategic use by diverse collectives and political spaces that include trans and queer activists but also other collectives that productively go beyond them. Following the *plebeya* (and even picaresque) strategy and reinterpretation of the juridical doctrine, the legal apparatus and, more generally, the state's agencies,[13] it is possible to foresee a shared setting for the right to identity, access to the public health system (including for lesbians, gays, sexual dissidents, and queers), and the wide range of associated rights. The LIG's proclamation of bodily autonomy as a sexual right, as well as access to public health systems, sets precedents for other cases. The so-called right to a respectful birth without surgical intervention and, at the time of this article's writing, the law of voluntary termination of pregnancy both exemplify feminist appropriations that have recourse to or can make use of the LIG. In this sense, one meeting point between subaltern and popular, queer, feminist, and sexually dissident subjects can be sewn around the use, appropriation, and instrumentalization of the LIG in its situatedness, in local contexts of structural inequality, the growth of poverty, and intensifying violence that have marred the recent Argentine stage. In effect, this poses a *plebeyo* use of the LIG that supports a possible alliance between both subjects without preconceived revolutionary or identitarian notions.

Martin De Mauro Rucovsky was part of the National Front for the Gender Identity Law and the "Incorporations" research team from 2008 to the present. He is currently a doctoral student at the National University of Córdoba, Argentina, and is the author of *Cuerpos en escena: Materialidad y cuerpo sexuado en Judith Butler y Paul B. Preciado* (2016; *Bodies on Scene: Materiality and Sexed Body in Judith Butler and Paul B. Preciado*).

Ian Russell is a PhD candidate in Brown University's Department of Hispanic Studies. His work focuses on transatlantic performance and queer temporalities.

Notes

1. *Sudaca* is a pejorative term used by Spaniards to refer to Latin Americans that has been reappropriated throughout Latin America's transition to a neoliberal and neocolonial economy as a means of signifying and reclaiming a marginalized (racially and economically) subject position within these power relations.—Translator

2. The use of the qualifier *trans* does not respond to the homogenizing use of the differences that distinguish identities, desires, and corporealities. "The term '*travesti*' in Latin America comes from the medical field and has been appropriated, re-elaborated, and embodied by the *travestis* themselves in an act of self-naming. This is the term by which we recognize ourselves and that we chose to construct ourselves as subjects of law. This process of appropriation of *travestismo* as a site from which we raise our voices and lay out our demands constitutes a political struggle" (Berkins 2008: 2–3).

3. The author of this article renders gendered nouns and adjectives with an asterisk (*), for example, "aliad*s," to disrupt the binaries that are built into language. This is difficult to reflect in English translation—I have opted for nongendered language—but should be noted as a fundamental attribute of the author's project within this essay.—Translator

4. The Yogyakarta Principles is a document about human rights in the areas of sexual orientation and gender identity, published as the outcome of an international meeting of human rights groups in Yogyakarta, Indonesia, in November 2006. The principles influenced the proposed UN declaration on sexual orientation and gender identity in 2008. The principles were supplemented in 2017 (the Yogyakarta Principles plus 10), expanding to include new grounds of gender expression and sex characteristics and a number of new principles.

5. By *popular subject* (popular position, popular pole, popular sectors), I am referring to mass sectors of society crossed by markers of class, race, gender, and ethnicity that are intimately tied up with structural inequalities. As well, rereading Ernesto Laclau and the tradition of populist thought in Latin America, *popular* refers to his impact in jointly articulating heterogeneous political and social demands.

6. This and all following citations of the Gender Identity Law itself are from Alejandra Sardá-Chandiramani and Radhika Chandiramani's original translation of the law

published by Global Action for Trans*Equality, available at tgeu.org/argentina
-gender-identity-law/.—Translator

7. Lohana Berkins (2008: 1), for her part, shows how the criminalization of *travesti* identity
    effected by the state through police edicts, minor, and misdemeanor codes restricted
    access to public space of various social groups—women working in prostitution, *car-
    tonerxs* (cardboard scavenger), *piqueterxs* (unemployed picketers), street vendors, and
    so on.

8. *Cissexual norm* refers to the limits of sexual difference that divide all identities and gender
    expressions into trans and nontrans. The distinctions among men, women, and trans-
    sexual persons functions on a logic of distribution that privileges the first two groups,
    while it fails to recognize the third (or recognizes it under the rule of a much smaller
    boundary). Cissexuality inverts the burden of proof by defining those subjects who lack
    the attribute of being trans.

9. The varied discursive registers that sedimented a eugenic position include the influx
    of the neo-Lamarkian tradition, Italian biotypology, German racial hygiene, the French
    physiognomic school, natalism, and pediatrics. The spread of these principles responded
    to the forms in which the elite classes conceived the problems of degeneration of pop-
    ulations of European origin living in the big urban centers of Latin America. In this
    context, some of the most prolific agents of Argentine eugenics (e.g., Enrique Díaz de
    Guijarro, Arturo Rossi, and Victor Delfino) founded distinct publications, forums, and
    even the first and only Department of Eugenics in the world, which ran from 1957
    through the 1980s under the tutelage of Carlos Bernardo de Quirós. See Miranda and
    Vallejo 2005.

10. Currently, some twenty European and Asian countries impose obligatory sterilization as
    a eugenic requirement in order to obtain legal recognition of gender identity. See the map
    of Transgender Europe (www.tgeu.org/sites/default/files/Trans_Map_Index_2014.pdf,
    accessed December 12, 2017) and the volume *Gender Is Not an Illness* (Sheherezade 2017).

11. The artists Roberto Jacoby and Syd Krochmalny created the installation *Newspapers
    of Hate* (*Diarios del odio*) that compile reader comments that appear in the online edition
    of the papers *La Nación* and *Clarín*. The exhibition was reinvented in 2016 in the form of
    poetry, with the same title.

12. On this point, I follow Carlos Figari (2016) with respect to a politics of allyship and
    coalitions as a method of struggle, collective work, and common agendas, just as we
    suggest in relation to the FNXLIG or the recently formed National Front for the Diana
    Sacayán Law.

13. Inspired by the work of thinker, poet, and activist Nestor Perlongher (1949–92), *plebeyo/a*
    refers to certain practices linked to popular culture, populist governments, and social
    activism. Based on the experiences of the marginalized, the lumpenproletariat, the
    downtrodden, the blasphemous, the contradictory, popular religious traditions, and a
    neobaroque aesthetic, *plebeyo/a* pertains to Latin America and, specifically, the Río de la
    Plata.

References

Berkins, Lohana. 2008. "Travestis: Una identidad política." In *La sexualidad represora*, 43–49.
    Buenos Aires: Topia.

Berkins, Lohana. 2007. *Cumbia, copeteo y lágrimas: Informe nacional sobre la situación de las
    travestis, transexuales y transgéneros.* Buenos Aires: Madres de Plaza de Mayo.

Berkins, Lohana, and Josefina Fernández. 2005. *La gesta del nombre propio: Informe sobre la situación de la comunidad travesti en la Argentina.* Buenos Aires: Madres de Plaza de Mayo.

Butler, Judith. 1990. *Gender Trouble: Feminism and the Subversion of Identity.* New York: Routledge.

Cabral, Mauro. 2012. "Algo ha pasado." In *Sexualidades, desigualdades y derechos*, edited by José Manuel Morán Faúndes, María Candelaria Sgró Ruata, and Juan Marco Vaggione, 251–73. Córdoba, Argentina: Edit/Ciencia, Derecho y Sociedad.

Celis, Mocha. 2017. *La revolución de las mariposas.* Buenos Aires: Publicación del Ministerio Público de la Defensa de la Ciudad Autónoma de Buenos Aires.

Cosecha Roja. 2016. "#ReconocerEsReparar la violencia institucional contra las personas trans." October 7. cosecharoja.org/reconoceresreparar-la-violencia-institucional-contra-las-personas-trans/.

De Mauro Rucovsky, Martín. 2015. "Trans* Necropolitics: Gender Identity Law in Argentina." *Sexualidad, Salud y Sociedad*, no. 20: 10–27. www.scielo.br/pdf/sess/n20/1984-6487-sess-20-0010.pdf.

Farji Neer, Anahí. 2017. *Travestismo, transexualidad y transgeneridad en los discursos del estado Argentino: Desde los edictos policiales hasta la Ley de Identidad de Género.* Buenos Aires: Teseo y Universidad de Buenos Aires Sociales.

Farji Neer, Anahí, and Ana Mines Cuenya. 2014. "Gubernamentalidad, despatologización y (des) medicalización: Interrogantes sobre la Ley de Identidad de Género Argentina (2011–2014)." *Século XXI: Revista de Ciências Sociais* 4, no. 2: 35–64.

Fernández, Josefina, Mónica D'Uva, and Paula Viturro, eds. 2008–9. *Políticas de reconocimiento.* 2 vols. Buenos Aires: Ají de pollo.

Figari, Carlos. 2012. "La identidad de género: Entre cortes y suturas." In *Derecho a la identidad de género: Ley n° 26.743*, coordinated by Carolina Von Opiela, 29–52. Buenos Aires: La Ley.

Figari, Carlos. 2016. "II. Queer Articulations." In *Critical Terms in Caribbean and Latin American Thought Historical and Institutional Trajectories*, edited by Yolanda Martínez-San Miguel, Ben Sifuentes-Jáuregui, and Marisa Belausteguigoitia, 231–38. New York: Palgrave Macmillan.

Litardo, Emiliano. 2013. "Los cuerpos desde ese otro lado: La Ley de Identidad de Género en Argentina." *Meritum* 8, no. 2: 227–55. www.fumec.br/revistas/meritum/article/view/2168.

Miranda, Marisa, and Gustavo Vallejo. 2005. *Darwinismo social y eugenesia en el Mundo Latino.* Buenos Aires: Siglo XXI.

Radi, Blas. 2013. "Algunas consideraciones sobre 'el binario' y la Ley de Identidad de Género en Argentina." Presentation at outreach event. www.aacademica.org/blas.radi/8.

Sabsay, Leticia. 2011. *Fronteras sexuales: Espacio urbano, cuerpos y ciudadanía.* Buenos Aires: Paidós.

Sheherezade, Kara. 2017. "Gender Is Not an Illness: How Pathologizing Trans People Violates International Human Rights Law." GATE. transactivists.org/wp-content/uploads/2017/12/Gender-is-not-an-illness-GATE-.pdf (accessed December 16, 2017).

Wayar, Marlene. 2012. "¿Qué pasó con la T?" *Suplemento Soy, Página/12*, May 11. www.pagina12.com.ar/diario/suplementos/soy/1-2436-2012-05-12.html.

Wayar, Marlene. 2010. "Intervención en la sesión simbólica." In *Legislatura de la Ciudad Autónoma de Buenos Aires: Día de lucha contra la discriminación por orientación sexual o identidad de género, 17 de mayo de 2010*, 31–32. circo-analisis.blogspot.com/2018/12/marlene-wayar-intervencion-en-la-sesion.html.

Giuseppe Campuzano's Afterlife

Toward a Travesti Methodology for Critique, Care, and Radical Resistance

MALÚ MACHUCA ROSE

Abstract The following hybrid essay contributes to, as well as complicates, the afterlife of Giuseppe Campuzano's work on *travesti* as methodology and offers questions raised from community organizing and collective care in order to claim a legacy of *travesti* as *curandera* (healer). This is made evident as the essay weaves through an affective history of AIDS-related struggles in life and death and the networks of care they invoke, including Campuzano's own, in order to move through questions of need, desire, collaboration, and urgency for gender and sexual dissidents in the Global South. These reflections result in a specific theorizing that challenges traditional forms knowledge production and creates possibilities through which to enact queer futures that enhance our commitment to one another's survival.

Keywords travesti, transfeminism, HIV/AIDS, necropolitics, critique

I write because my *ancestras* work moves me in such a way that I must take responsibility for continuing to ask the questions they began to trace. Not just that—I must ask new ones. I write because *ser travesti* is not just about gender or sexuality. *Es una fiesta, mi amor.*[1] It's about daring to transgress, to open up new possibilities. I write as a way to fight for our future, to stress the responsibility we have to one another in our collective care and in our scholarly artist-activist work. I write because of my commitment to my community's lives, even when death has already taken over. I write because I hope to enact here the creative, politico-theoretical exploration of what we and our work mean to one another, to write *with* the communities I'm a part of. I write to move us toward a future imagined by our *ancestras*, which can be felt and enacted by us.[2] I ask, What does it mean to be undone by another's loss, death, the very reality of our precarious lives, in ways that move us spiritually, creatively, critically toward a different

TSQ: Transgender Studies Quarterly ★ Volume 6, Number 2 ★ May 2019
DOI 10.1215/23289252-7348524 © 2019 Duke University Press

understanding of ourselves?[3] How does an intimacy with travesti death affect our imagining and building of our political community in the face of indescribable, sometimes even ungrievable loss?[4]

In the last fifteen years, the diva that is Giuseppe Campuzano rose to public attention, both in Peru and internationally, because of her scholarly artistic work that led to the art installation and book project she named *Museo Travesti del Perú* (*Travesti Museum of Peru*; Campuzano 2007). *Absoluta, absolutísima!*[5] Her project seduced many, in part because it reflected a longing to see queerness written into our indigenous history, and in part because the images she produced were transgressive, counterhistorical, and beautiful. It also provided many of us, sexual and gender dissidents, with a vision of ourselves that did not compromise our roots, or our faggotry—a vision that never needed to be absolutely redeemable, uncomplicated, or without contradiction.

Miguel A. López, scholar-curator and a friend of Giuseppe, described the *Museo Travesti del Perú* as "halfway between performance and historical research," situated in a promiscuous intersectional thinking of history through the perspective of "a fictional figure he calls the androgynous indigenous/mixed-race transvestite" or, more specifically, *travesti* (López and Campuzano 2013). The *Museo Travesti del Perú* uses a multiplicity of artifacts of *travestismo*—photos, clothes, crafts, and objects—to confront and challenge the colonized vision of the nation-state and fracture heterosexual subjectivity, giving possibility to "invisible subjects whose life is permanently between life and death: the HIV-positive, the undocumented immigrants, the intersex."

The implications of this project, then, go far beyond narrow conceptions of trans or gender studies, as it embodies a critique of an entire mode of scientific Western knowledge production that has attempted to speak for and about our bodies, our communities, and our histories. Giuseppe's self-fashioned methodology is completely promiscuous, invented through the body as a site for reinvention and the creation of a truth that is as artificial as the limits that produced its erasure. To quote *la cabra* herself,[6] speaking of a piece in the museum that consisted of a pair of worn-down white platform heels named *La Carlita*, which she almost lost after an installation in Bogotá:

> My friend Carla migrated from Peru to Italy in 2003. She was getting rid of some things, among them a pair of old shoes, so I asked her to give them to me. . . . She always offered to send me a new pair and I repeated that I kept those as an allegory for her travels (transgender, transnational). Carlita was murdered in 2008 by a john. In 2009 I looked for the shoes once more, this time to take them to Bogotá but I could not find them: my mother had thrown them in the garbage! After a hysterical fetishist moment, I managed to recover its travesti meaning and I simply

got another pair. That falsified Carlita was the one you gave me back, that I pruned, as a symbol of a truncate trip, to show it at la Trienal de Chile, at the Museum of Contemporary Art in Santiago. The original Carlita never existed. (La Fountain-Stokes, n.d.)

It is in this spirit that I write this to speak not only about Campuzano and the Travesti Museum but also about *mi familia infecta*: the families we create out of our impure blood, our abject bodies, and undesirable fluids. I write because I need to speak about ancestrality, the meaning of legacy, the ways in which we write ourselves not just into history but into our communities. I write to contribute to the field of queer of color critique, but one that is rooted in *cuerpas/territorias* (body/territories) from the Global South.

I also write even when the knowledge I have to share openly defies academic translation, not just because our indigenous tongues have been, largely, taken from us with the imposition of Spanish first, and English second, but because it is sacred knowledge, unable to be fully known or understood under the current paradigms that dominate our fields and the intellectual spaces we produce knowledge from. So there may be some things here that will be messy, unexplainable, unverifiable, unscientific, unable to be categorized—and that is part of the message. Attempting to know everything is a colonial epistemology in which I refuse to be complicit.

Even though this essay states my affiliation with a university and my status as a graduate student, I am writing first and foremost as the child of the *campesinas* that the terrorist state was unable to sterilize. I am here as the child of the travestis that refuse to be killed even when their physical bodies are no longer here. I am here as an activist who has been working on the ground for over ten years, as an artist who is struggling to find their voice, as a scholar who is both hypervisible and unable to be truly seen, and as a healer evoking magic and collective power. Most important, I am writing as a hot ass mess, as a *loca, maricón, travesti, chuquichinchay, bebita furiosa, gordx rabiosx, escandalosa, impertinente, deseosa, chismosa, qariwarmi, guerrerx,* and *bruja*.

I came to know about the work Giuseppe was doing through my *tío*, Germain Machuca, my father's younger sibling.[7] For me, as a child, he was always my favorite, the one who moved their body like no one else, who constantly transformed their body—and mine—in ways I was just starting to dream possible. Since age three, she would bring me in her room and say I was her favorite model. I would beg her, "Píntameee" (paint my face), and she would ask to be acknowledged in her beauty before she would accept. Once I had sufficiently complimented her, telling her how perfect, beautiful, wonderful, stunning, gorgeous she is, we would begin. I remember that trance-like emotion when I would feel his soft hands working their magic on me, feeling their breathing on my face as they shared with me the sacred, dangerous, thrilling, and extremely pleasurable world of dying in front of the mirror to be reborn as *Otra*, to lend your body to another, to connect to our *ancestras travestis*, to become one of the multiple possibilities that inhabit one's *cuerpa/territoria*. Many times, she has birthed me. I have always been her child. She has always been *mi hada madrina*, my fairy godmother. In the stories she has told me over the years, she always repeats how they met all their soul mates and lovers in front of a mirror. I think this is how we fell in love, too. I cannot think of another moment more defining for the *maricón* that I am today.

Mi tío Germain and Giuseppe were connected through a lifeline of blood and semen, infectious fluids carrying both danger and pleasure, creating our own deadly bloodlines and families along the way, moving through bodies as a bio-hazardous sexual threat. They met as teens during the eighties, at the height of the civil war, the HIV/AIDS crisis, and state-imposed curfews in Peru: just two tall queens in a club way too small for their egos. The ways in which they are connected and disconnected from each other are complicated and deeply personal, but it is important that you know that even though a lot of their travesti work has been done together, only one of them has the international recognition that they both deserve.

TRAVEEEEEEESTIIIIIII!!! MARICOOOOOOOOÓN!!!! CABRIIIIÍSII-MAAAAAAAAA!!!

The word *travesti* functions in Campuzano's work not as an identity but as a methodology and epistemology. Giuseppe's use of *travesti* is not without tension. In Peru, an important part of the trans movement rejects the use of the word, reminding us of its history as a derogatory term that is used to delegitimize trans women as women. The investment in *trans* as an umbrella term for the multiple indigenous forms of gender and sexual dissidence stems, very clearly in my opinion, from the need to be seen, validated, and most important, funded by people in power from the Global North—those who have the power to make our government listen and obey under the threat of isolation from the globalized neoliberal capitalist order. In contrast to the supposed universality of *trans*, *travesti* is provincialized and particular, even where some form of this word exists in many languages. The most obvious definition of *travesti* comes from the verb *travestir*, to cross-dress. Hence, the travesti is the body that cross-dresses and becomes a type of person, the travesti subject. Travesti is not woman and is not trans. Travesti is classed and raced: it means you do not present femininely all of the time because you cannot afford to. It means the use of body technologies to transform one's body does not come from a doctor's office but from resource-fulness in the face of *precarización*, the act by which the matrix of domination makes our bodies and our lives precarious. *¿Más clarito?* It means you get creative, you use pens for eyeliner, get your hormones and silicones from your friends underground, or use *tinta* instead of *testosterona* to transform your body. It also means you're only safe at night, when the children are sleeping and the darkness allows a certain freedom and permissiveness to roam more freely, to perform gender and sexuality with less judgment, outside the scrutiny of the regular order, state agents, and the establishment. Travesti is usually a sex worker, whether out of need for money, validation, survival, or most likely a mixture of the three. She does not have a DNI, Documento Nacional de Identificación—most likely she never has had one. She is undocumented, and most of the time she has migrated away from the family she was birthed into in order to be reborn among those of her kind. Travesti is the refusal to be trans, the refusal to be woman, the refusal to be intelligible.

Most important, she has always been here. The central aim of Campuzano's travesti project is not to find the travestis in Peruvian history but, rather, to make out of her travesti body a map, a museum, an epistemology, to create on her body a way of coming to know the world and to weave oneself into it. It is about using *nuestra mariconada y nuestro escándalo, tomar ese exceso que también es chisme con labial, escarcha y risa de loca*, to destabilize the colonial nation-state project, its history, its ideals, its methods, and its narratives. We are drawing a line that connects us to the ancestors the colonizers tried to erase, and we will not be complicit in this killing of our bodies/territories when, as travestis we stand in our power as sacred beings, shamans, and witches able to cross between the spheres of masculine and feminine energy, thus being closer to the divine, that realm of *danza/batalla* (dance/battle) and *peligro/poder* (danger/power) that ultimately triggers transformation.[8]

When we claim ourselves as part of this sacred tradition we are tapping into a form of power that is routinely displaced from us but also given to us through the history of the treatment of our bodies. The fact that we simultaneously cause so much social anxiety, lust, and distress is the key that, in this project of travesti as a politics, we are trying to claim for ourselves. Our power comes from living on the edge, the margins, *la calle*, the hours between dawn. Our power comes from tapping into the sacred space of transcendence, the refusal to accept coherence, stability, or respectability as a way of life. To stand in this refusal, when so many cannot and will not see us as human and will not honor the power we are trying to claim for ourselves, also puts us at risk.

This is where I want to intervene my right to complicate Campuzano's project in order to visualize new potentialities, a way of moving her critique forward as we attempt to fill the spaces that she left when she passed away in 2013. I claim her as my *ancestra* as I claim the right to do a critique of her work, which demands of me the capability to see her contributions as well as her shortcomings and to claim those as opportunities for growing in her legacy as we create one of our own; to do a reading that is travesti, critical and tender, reparative but sharp; to do with *ternura radical*, because this work is important and political and intimate; to do the asking and challenging as we care for one another and acknowledge our fragilities and differences as sites of resistance, imagination, and politico-affective agency (D'Emilia 2015). I want to ask what it means to do work in the afterlife of somebody whose impact has been so critical and has moved and inspired us toward new collaborations with one another. So many young *cabritas* have been brought together by the impact of her work, the grief and loss after her passing. Most of us have articulated a sense of urgency to be with each other in different ways, after her death, and the deaths of those in our communities who have continued to die after her passing. The work I have been doing over the past five years has included the creation of performance art pieces, documentary theater plays, community-based research projects, publishing books, and collecting oral histories from over a thousand *cabras* all over Peru. It has also involved loving and caring for my community, my friends, lovers, *bebitas*, sometimes even strangers. Some days, some of the most important work I have done has been cooking, dancing, drinking, listening, opening up my home, and providing warmth and nurture.

After her death, conversations surrounding Campuzano's HIV/AIDS politics have been less present than during the time she was actively working on these issues. Giuseppe embraced HIV infection as a crucial and provocative form of power, in the ways in which it allowed us to create a bloodline of queers and dissidents: a new blood family out of impurity, in ways that threaten notions of biological, heteronormative families. *El cache*, sex, our own fucking and our desire, are brought back to the front and center of our political and intellectual work. To examine what desire provokes in terms of our gender, what it produces in our embodiments, the ways in which we are moved by others for whom we feel erotic connections, which may very well be untamable and ungovernable emotion—that which by definition makes us queer. It is our methodology, a space for us to enact the unthinkable, undreamable, *lo irrespetable, impensable e, incluso, grotesco*. We never had to fuck pretty because we were already travesti, *maricón*. We needed the theory to understand this position as powerful, in that it destabilizes that which is deemed as respectable knowledge on human sexuality and gender. This way of fucking, living, being, looking, and performing travesti disrupts norms, is chaotic by nature, unrestricted, high risk, and high reward. Giuseppe's proposition of power over an HIV-seropositive status and the travesti body threatens parts of the gay and trans community who would rather see themselves disaligned from the stigma of a death still associated with promiscuity, immorality, undesirability, untouchability.

In Latin America, Peru is one of the few countries that have not yet formulated laws that are affirmative or protective of the queer and transgender
population (No Tengo Miedo 2016). Violence against queers, and particularly
mariconas escandalosas, is not only sanctioned by the nation-state through the
lack of access to justice but also perpetuated through law enforcement person-
nel, who target working-class trans and gender-nonconforming folks for sexual
harassment, rape, arbitrary detention, and beatings, among others (Instituto Runa
2006). Furthermore, the HIV/AIDS crisis has deeply affected the negotiation for
recognition from the state. With the first case of HIV reported in 1983, it was
only in 1996 that the state implemented a structured program, with budgeted
resources, to prevent HIV/AIDS targeting specific at-risk populations and providing antiretroviral treatment for mother-to-child transmission (Cueto 2002). It
was not until 2004, more than twenty years after the first case, that a program to
provide universal access to antiretroviral treatment was made available by the
Ministry of Health (Ministerio de Salud del Perú 2006). This reveals that no care
is provided by the state when people are characterized as responsible for the causes
of their death and their own violence—or, rather, that the only way in which care
is provided is if sexual and gender dissidents let go of those behaviors, sexual
practices, aesthetics, and relationships that make their life queer, and therefore
worth living. What does it mean, then, to ask for care and survival, standing in
refusal to live a life of a sanitized existence, sex life, politics?[9]

It is because of all the possibilities that I see stemming from Campuzano's
work that I am pushed to think about new ways of asking her questions even in
death: Where is the place of collaboration and friendship in her project before and
after she became disabled? How many of these ideas and explorations in gender
and travesti performance were done in *complicidad* with others? Why do we need
others when we are faced with death and not with recognition? Who influences
our work even when nobody knows their name? Who do we find out that we need
in death that we could not acknowledge in life? How does death structure our
relationships to one another's survival?

I started spending more time with her when she fell ill and her death was
imminent. Even then, she generously provided space for me to interview her and
share my research with her. She asked me to share more about disability studies
as she was beginning to write a different kind of body into her performance-
scholarly work. Giuseppe Campuzano passed away in November 2013 after a long
battle with HIV/AIDS-related lipodystrophy and amyotrophic lateral sclerosis,
which made her body extremely vulnerable and thus caused her to need her friends
and chosen family even more. Becoming crip, developing a hunger and a need for
disability studies, and attempting to weave that into her work were all peaking
when she passed.

A lot of her work, and the recognition that came with it, would not have been possible without a network of talented artists and researchers who helped piece together the project of travesti that she ultimately authored. It is likely that a lot of scholars work that way, but for me and my community of *bebitas furiosas* who are attempting to build a transfeminist politics from the Global South,[10] being together and creating collectively are not just preferred but needed, to cite one another as we create together as well as individually, to reference where the ideas we are taking credit for are imagined collectively. To give credit where being recognized by others is a form of survival has become a key practice in ensuring everyone's work, whether intellectual, emotional, physical, or domestic, is valued, acknowledged, seen, and understood, but also interpreted and infused with value and meaning. Whose work are we building on when we are making sense of a world we experience and transform together? Whom do we erase in our work in order to insert others who are already so often acknowledged? Who, if not the community of *cabras* I am surrounded with, informs the way in which I theorize my social existence? And most important, what kind of knowledge gets valued and devalued as we move forward in creating a community-based artist/scholarly/political practice?

We held the most beautiful funeral for *la mariconíxima*.[11] My *tío* Germain lent her his body, and we had a *pasacalle* throughout her block, with a band singing both *A quién le importa*, by Alaska y Dinarama, and *Que linda flor, qué hermosa flor*, a popular Andean *huayno* song. She was that, *una cholita travesti*.[12] I had never been at a travesti funeral before, but I have had to hold many since she passed. For me, coming to a trans and nonbinary identity has also signified a politics of community, of impure bloodlines and legacies, of healing and caring for each other as political work. This is Germain's legacy, which is hidden in Giuseppe's work, and which I also claim for myself. As a child in the late 1980s and 1990s, Germain took care of many of her friends who died at the height of the AIDS epidemic, creating a sense of devotion and healing that I believe to be central to the identity of travesti as *curandera*. Germain has been for many decades now *la curandera que* provides nurture, care, and healing in so many of our *ancestras'* most vulnerable moments. She did this early on for *las locas del* Teatro del Sol, Peru's first *teatro maricón*, where she was adopted by Beto Montalva and Pipo Ormeño, to learn theater, dance, performance, after she had found a photograph of them in the newspaper and ran after school to see their play. She also learned about the pain in our deaths and our struggles to survive. She fought for Pipo *y* Beto to have a hospital bed in the times when even money could not buy you health care for HIV/AIDS. She cared for Giuseppe and has done so for many others over the years.[13]

The centrality of this work as a travesti politics has become painfully evident during the past five years as I have become a full-time activist working on the ground. As Lohana Berkins (2014), queen of *furia* travesti, would say: "After marriage equality passed in Argentina, you would think that our boyfriends would go running claiming social security for their travesti wives, but it has not happened. They do not want to take us out of the dark. Nothing has changed for us."

Yefri Peña is an iconic travesti from *el Cono Este de Lima* who, a little over ten years ago, survived one of the most gruesome hate crimes in Peruvian history. She was attacked by five men who took off her silicone breasts, broke her arms, left her bleeding out on the streets in front of a police van. She had to pay one hundred soles to get a taxi to drive her to the hospital. They did not want to touch her there, refused to wipe the sweat of her forehead or give her water. They left her for dead; she struggled to show she was alive. She was released the next day alleging lack of space for her at the hospital. She spent one month at her house sitting on a chair without food, water, or an IV. After twenty-eight days she woke up and said, "Mamá, tengo sed," and drank two liters of water in one sitting. She is the most powerful, strongest person I know. She has since then gotten back on the streets, working as a peer sex-health educator, taking several travesti sex workers to get regular checkups, buying them food, providing space to talk, to laugh, for *chisme* and for counsel.[14] For this she is both loved and feared at every health care center she visits. She will not allow for any discrimination toward another travesti. And she will always leave with the most condoms in her purse. So, when she calls, you just answer. Me and Rudi *y* Adriana, my intense and beautiful research *compañeras*, were pulling together our second book when Yefri called us crying at the beginning of 2016 because one of her friends, Yuya, had fallen ill due to AIDS-related health issues, as well as tuberculosis. The doctors at Hospital Hipólito Unanue en El Agustino refused to see her. We left everything to go raise hell for them. For a year we took care of Yuya through a list of volunteers to see her and feed her when she was unable to, since the hospital would not. We ran a campaign to crowdsource funds for her care *y armamos un ESCÁNDALO* so the hospital would admit her. After about a year of in-hospital treatment, she recovered and was on her way to getting out of there when she relapsed and suddenly passed away. It took us several hours to retrieve her body from the hospital, as they would not recognize we were family, even when I had been signing all of her consent forms for the past year. At the hospital morgue, they would not touch her. They wanted to sell her body to medical students, to whom the hospital gave my number and who would not stop calling and harassing me, saying that we were selfish for not "contributing to science" and that they would bury the body after they were done anyway. We said no, even when we could barely afford her burial. I said, "No—you have taken enough from us through your actions and omissions. Let her community give our Yuya a proper burial." We had to go in and get her cold body from the hospital morgue freezer, clean her, dress her, and organize her wake. We bought her a dress, and I did her makeup. Even dead, she was looking very *coqueta*, just as she did when I met her, unable to speak yet picking husbands from her hospital bed, sorting through all the cute boys roaming the halls. "Porque ser travesti es una fiesta, mi amor." At the wake, only four people showed up. I think most people who identified with her were scared about what this meant for their own mortality. She always talked about multiple boyfriends whom she loved and literally gave her life for, but none of them were there. Yefri called *y PUTEÓ A TODO EL MUNDO* and told them that they needed to come, that it could have been any of us.[15] And then travestis from all over *el Cono Este* came to her funeral. We talked about how *nos desvivimos por el hombre*, we lust so much to be desired back by these men who refuse to acknowledge us publicly, and that's ultimately what kills us. Patriarchy is killing us. We cannot keep looking to men for care. We need to care in our own travesti ways.

I want to think about what it means to acknowledge oneself in intimacy with the vulnerability that makes travesti life marked for death, what it means to move inside and out of that level of risk, to ask if care will be forfeited from us when we most need it. In the face of extreme violence, as Jina B. Kim theorized in her talk "Cripping the Welfare Queen" (2018), interdependency moves us from a stigmatized position onto a radical crip-of-color mutual need of others for survival, which becomes crucial for creating a livable world. I bare the question, What does interdependency mean in light of a necropolitical state whose HIV/AIDS politics sees *locas, travestis y putas* as responsible for their own deaths? How does the death of others with whom one identifies—who are not yet recognized as grievable—produce new forms of interdependency and care among the living, the living-dead, and the dead?

Before Giuseppe passed, she organized an intricate network of care and support, including multiple friends who assisted her when she was no longer able to move on her own. She never wanted to be a burden to her biological mother, but in a way she believed that it was up to us as an impure family to care for one another. This is where I want to pick up on her work, on the centrality of collaboration as a liberatory practice, as a deeply travesti practice now embodied in myself and the *bebitas* around me.

A couple summers ago, Max Lira, Ibrain Plácido, and I opened an artistic laboratory under the name Bebitas Furiosas: Deseos Peligrosos (Lira Tapia, Machuca Rose, and Plácido San Martín 2016), a space for different *cabritas, travestis, bebitas, y mariconas* to explore different techniques and technologies in order to collectively research, create, dance, heal, liberate, feel erotic, experience wellness and freedom. The three of us came to know one another and to offer our vulnerability to one another through a common sensitivity regarding Giuseppe's work, *una capacidad de movernos y conmovernos*, a capacity to move and be moved that we believed could take us to deeper explorations of that impure travesti positionality. To explore travesti as an epistemological possibility to be something beyond man or woman, gay or straight, but that is still *loca* and, maybe most important, brown, *precarizada*, already existing in the margin and making that a beautiful place to be. Yefri, Yuya, Giuseppe, and Germain are all travestis we claim as ancestors because of the multiple possibilities in the practices of creating a world where we can exist. Furthermore, Giuseppe's legacy is not only in the brilliance and excellence in her scholarship, in the rigor in her research, or in her creativity and self-expression. It is also in her vulnerability, in her needing her friends, in the structures that feed into the narcissistic self that allows so many scholars to speak from the I but that for us, for the legacy we are claiming, is a constant turn to the collective. To the community, to *las amigas*, to *las bebitas furiosas*, to the ways in which we see ourselves, we heal ourselves, we hurt and nurture each other.

     I think of the parties we hold to celebrate one another often, the meals we cook together, the joints we smoke, the way in which we create the most fabulous outfits and personas out of precarious conditions, how creativity and resourcefulness rise in the face of marginality and urgency. I think of the strategies we navigate to become who we are in spaces we fight more and more to create for ourselves. I think of La Casita Transfeminista that held so many parties and study sessions, wine downs, and activist meetings, writings of books and relationships, good sex and bad sex, fearing for our lives and our safety, and also rejoicing in our accomplishments together, even when it's been the most difficult. I think of Casa Bagre, Chola Contravisual, Serena Morena, PGNBebxs, La Munay, La Promesa, Trenzar, the work of Ashanti, de Diversidades Trans Masculinas, of the people at Bisagra, Dulce Fanzín, No Tengo Miedo, Acción Crítica, Imaginario Colectivo, Hijas de Lilith, Pussy Fiesta, Bésame Pasiva, el FRAX, and many other spaces we have created under multiple names in order to find ourselves in community. I think of all the ways in which we have strived to celebrate those who are most endangered within our communities. I think of *la cuerpita de la Fabrizia, bailando* and running to my room for an outfit change before the night is over, both outshining and inspiring everybody else. I think of Mayu, *la Wawita Absoluta*, creating beautiful art and educating with tenderness in the face of so much violence. I think of Pau Flores and her devotion to HIV/AIDS work even when she was dying of this herself. I think of Paloma Martinez and the need, the urgency for validation. I think of our parties, *la escarcha, los brillitos y los puntos*. I think of this complicated legacy and the tension between the personal and the collective, between whom we fuck and whom we are friends with, between *nuestra pulsión de vida y de muerte*, the eros and the thanatos, if you will.

I go back to our sacred space of healing together as a form of fighting for a future that has always been ours, even when we are constantly denied the opportunity to continue living. *Museo Travesti del Perú* has meant, in Giuseppe's afterlife, a project that for many of us has signified not only a looking at the past but also a longing and searching toward a queer futurity. As Giuseppe herself said, "El potencial del Museo Travesti no equivale a la cantidad o el costo de su colección, sino a su audacia para deconstruir y replantear continuamente sus supuestos" (The Travesti Museum's potential is not in the quantity or cost of its collection but, rather, its audacity to deconstruct and constantly challenge its suppositions) (Campuzano 2008: 50). Travesti now, for *las bebitas*, functions as a doorway that allows us to dream of a past connected to a future that can be enacted by celebrating the abundance of racialized and *sudaca* travesti aesthetics, sensitivities, and desires while drawing from an infectious lineage that connects us to our ancestors and our *muertas* who lived before us, no matter how validated their contributions are by the academic world.

Cuando una travesti muere, nunca muere. Giuseppe Campuzano y Yuya Romayna, presente. When a travesti dies, she never dies. Giuseppe Campuzano and Yuya Romayna, present.

Malú Machuca Rose is a graduate student in the Department of Gender and Women's Studies at the University of Wisconsin–Madison. Their research focuses on trans and queer death and survival, nightlife, sex and risk, feminism, critical theory, art, and healing justice. They have coauthored *Nuestra Voz Persiste* (2016) and *Estado de Violencia* (2014) as part of their work in the No Tengo Miedo collective in Lima, Peru.

Acknowledgments

Nobody has been more fundamental to this work than Germain Machuca, whose love, guidance, and infinite conversations have definitively shaped my life. I am indebted to my activist community, which continues to support me and hold me accountable, namely, Max Lira, Bertha Prieto, Milagros Olivera, Selva Félix, Ibrain Plácido, Brunella Landi, Rudi Cocchella, Adriana Gallegos, Marco Pérez, Yefri Peña, and Eme Eyzaguirre. This work would not have been possible without committed and rigorous feedback from professors Chris Barcelos and Jill Casid, as well as invaluable contributions by Finn Enke and Ramzi Fawaz. Thank you to GiuCamp and her family and friends, who have believed in me since I started writing about her, especially Miguel López, Susana Torres, and Karen Bernedo. Finally, this work has been refined by the scholar community formed at our Necrocene, Necropolitics, Necrolandscaping seminar in the spring of 2018, as well as the UCLA QGrad Conference in 2017, where I initially presented an earlier version of this article. Zitlaly Mendoza, I will never forget your tears (and mine) during that first day. Special thanks to Chris Cañete Rodriguez, Ellie Hayden, and Anders Zanichknowsky for their brilliant comments, friendship, and support during this time. Yuya, Pau, Paloma, Duda, Quincy and Zuleymi, Fabrizio, Mica, Lia, and Tahiel: this is for you.

Notes

1. *Me robo* this phrase from a piece by the same name written by Camila Sosa Villada (2016), travesti militant artist from Argentina.

2. I write inspired by the legacy of womxn of color and queer and trans people of color using autoethnography and autotheory to explore, narrate, and enact our different truths through art and other forms of cultural production. I'm particularly inspired by the work of Jillian Hernández (2018) in exploring the meaning of mourning and aesthetics for Latinx femmes through autoethnographic prose that brings the reader into contact with the author's grandmother.

3. Here I am thinking with Judith Butler's work in *Undoing Gender* (2004), questioning what death does or undoes for those who are connected and committed to one another's lives, recognition, and justice. I'm also moving through these questions with Butler's writing in *Frames of War* (2009), as I identify travesti lives to be particularly precarious under the necropolitical Peruvian state.

4. This set of questions are inspired by multiple conversations with Jill H. Casid over the spring of 2018, with and around the work of Stuart J. Murray in "Thanatopolitics: On the Use of Death for Mobilizing Political Life" (2006: 195), which frames a politics of death as a "response and a resistance to biopolitical power and to the Western conception of rational sovereignty with which biopolitics is allied." This understanding of death as a political act has important connotations on my urgency to theorize intimacy with travesti death as its connected to multiple affective, rhetorical, and symbolic devices through which travesti life and survival are produced.

5. *Absoluta!* is an exclamation that comes from old *telenovelas*, which my *tío* Germain taught me and which is a part of the way we talk to each other. *Cuando la mala de la novela* walks in looking fabulous, even though her whole character is based on a dilemma, she would be *absoluta*, overcoming aesthetically her dramatic position. "Absoluta!," we exclaim to each other, too, when we overcome with fabulosity.

6. *Cabra* is a term that comes from the insult *cabro*, which literally translates to "goat," meaning faggot. *Cabra* is the feminized form of the insult, a term reclaimed and used to encompass different forms of sexual and gender dissidence that move toward faggotry, *mariconada*, with an in-your-face attitude. It includes multiple genders, sexualities and bodies that move toward that form of feeling, and it is used intimately, among friends and *bebitas*.

7. Throughout this article, I use multiple gender pronouns to refer both to Germain and Giuseppe. I use this as a resource to destabilize gender categories as this is how I usually talk about them in Spanish as well. Germain would say to me, "I tried pants, I tried skirts—and I can't stick to either of them!"

8. These ideas on gender and de/colonization are affirmed in Campuzano's work through the scholarship of Michael Horswell (2005, referenced here as the Spanish version published in 2013).

9. The idea of travestis and *maricas* refusing to live a sanitized existence in regard to sex as a radical politics of desire is inspired by Néstor Perlongher's writing on *las locas* as a subject with a nomad sexuality that transcends "not only the heterosexual order, but is also a marginal position in the homosexual movement, in contrast to the masculine middle-class gay, whose place as a model citizen is central to the visibility and assimilationist politics sustained by the gay movement from the 80s and on" (Davis 2012).

10. *Bebitas furiosas* is deployed as a gender category to signify vulnerability, childlike play, a claiming of gender akin to femme, a softness, *un ser pasiva* that is also furious, angry, upset, disturbed. This concept was created as a collaboration among Max Lira, Ibrain Plácido, and myself—all nonbinary *cabras cholitxs* trying to ground our explorations surrounding desire in our aesthetic practice.

11. *Mariconíxima* is a play on words used by Germain and Giuseppe, meaning the most maricón, and it's also used in this piece to gesture toward the title of an article I wrote and published online immediately after Giuseppe's death, on her legacy, our connection, and the impact of her beautiful travesti funeral, called "Mariconíxima renace en cabrísimo ritual" (Machuca Rose 2013).

12. *Cholita* is a diminutive from the term *chola*, used as a form of endearment. *Chola* in Peru is a racial category that signals indigenous people and people of indigenous descent who have migrated from the mountains, *la sierra* (often pejoratively called *serranxs*) into the city. In a country where most brown people deem themselves *mestizx* (mixed) as a form of eluding indigeneity, *cholx* works as a slur to remind the bearers of their origins. It has also been made into a verb: *cholear* means to racialize somebody, to minimize and put them in their place by naming that they are *cholx* (Avilés 2017).

13. I'm currently working on a follow-up article to this one, centering intimacy with HIV/AIDS as read through the lens of disability, curative violence, folded temporalities, care work, and interdependence, as well as with and against the life and legacy of Germain Machuca.

14. Yefri Peña has also since been attacked again, as recently as December 7, 2018. She was going to get bread from the *panadería*, a couple blocks away from her home in Ate Vitarte, the *barrio* where she's lived for most of her life, when she was assaulted by a man who broke open her skull as he screamed transphobic insults. She has not yet gotten justice for either one of these attacks.

15. The word *puteó* comes from the verbo *putear*, which can be literally translated to "to slut." It has many meanings. In this context, *putear* means to speak assertively to put things in order, usually with the use of slurs and slang, in order to be understood in a demanding code that also shows closeness and mutual commitment to one another. For example, it's often done in parenting. When people respond and allow themselves to be *puteadas* by Yefri, they assert that she was ultimately right to call them out for not being present and therefore immediately show up, as a sign of respect, love, care, and a reaffirmation to this commitment.

References

Avilés, Marco. 2017. *No soy tu cholo*. Lima: Penguin Random House.

Berkins, Lohana. 2014. "¿Casarse? ¿Nosotras? ¡Sí! ¿Para qué?: Aventuras y desventuras de antiguas y futuras bodas través." *Página/12*, July 18. www.pagina12.com.ar/diario/suplementos/soy/1-3534-2014-07-18.html.

Butler, Judith. 2004 "Besides Oneself: On the Limits of Sexual Autonomy." In *Undoing Gender*, 17–39. New York: Routledge.

Butler, Judith. 2009. "Precarious Life, Grievable Life." In *Frames of War: When Is Life Grievable?*, 1–32. London: Verso.

Campuzano, Giuseppe. 2007. *Museo travesti del Perú*. Lima: author's edition, with the support of the Institute of Development Studies.

Campuzano, Giuseppe. 2008. "El Museo Travesti del Perú." *Decisio*, no. 20: 49–53.

Cueto, Marcos. 2002. "El rastro del SIDA en el Perú." *História, Ciências, Saúde—Manguinhos*, no. 9: 17–40.

Davis, Fernando. 2012. "La micropolítica deseante de Néstor Perlongher." *Micropolíticas de la desobediencia sexual en el arte contemporáneo*, November 8. micropoliticasdesobediencia sexualarte.blogspot.com/2012/11/devenir-loca.html.

D'Emilia, Dani. 2015. "Encarnando la ternura radical: Alianzas político-afectivas y descoloniza-ción del cuerpo en la performance-pedagogía de la pocha nostra." Master's thesis, Museu d'Art Contemporani de Barcelona, Universidad Autònoma Barcelona.

Hernández, Jillian. 2018. "Beauty Marks: The Latinx Surfaces of Loving, Becoming, and Mourning." *Women and Performance* 28, no. 1: 67–84.

Horswell, Michael. 2013. *La descolonización del sodomita en los Andes coloniales.* Quito: Abya Yala Ediciones.

Instituto Runa. 2006. *Realidades invisibles: Violencia contra travestis, transexuales y transgéneros que ejercen comercio sexual en la ciudad de Lima.* Lima: Instituto Runa.

Kim, Jina B. 2018. "Cripping the Welfare Queen—Disability and Race in the Afterlife of U.S. Welfare Reform." Keynote speech given at "Bodies of Resistance: Second Annual UW Gender and Women's Studies Symposium," University of Wisconsin–Madison, March 2.

La Fountain-Stokes, Lawrence. n.d. "Giuseppe Campuzano y El Museo Travesti del Peru." Hemispheric Institute, *E-misférica*. hemisphericinstitute.org/hemi/es/campuzano-entrevista (accessed February 3, 2018).

Lira Tapia, Max, Malú Machuca Rose, and Ibrain Plácido San Martín. 2016. "Bebitas Furiosas // Deseos Peligrosos." www.facebook.com/events/1000242570018613/ (accessed February 3, 2018).

López, Miguel A., and Giuseppe Campuzano. 2013. "Reality Can Suck My Dick, Darling: The Museo Travesti del Perú and the Histories We Deserve." *Visible: Workbook 2.* www .visibleproject.org/blog/the-museo-travesti-del-peru-and-the-histories-we-deserve-by -giuseppe-campuzano-and-miguel-lopez/.

Machuca Rose, Malú. 2013. "Mariconíxima renace en cabrísimo ritual: De cómo enterramos a la Virgen Santísima de todas las Cabras, Giuseppe Campuzano." *La Mula Feministas*, November 12. feministas.lamula.pe/2013/11/12/mariconixima-renace-en-cabrisimo-ritual /malulin/.

Ministerio de Salud del Perú. 2006. *Un paso adelante en la lucha contra el sida: Los primeros dos años de Acceso Universal al tratamiento antirretroviral en el Perú.* Lima: Ministerio de Salud del Perú.

Murray, Stuart J. 2006. "Thanatopolitics: On the Use of Death for Mobilizing Political Life." *Polygraph*, no. 18: 191–215.

No Tengo Miedo. 2016. *Nuestra voz persiste: Diagnóstico de la situación de personas lesbianas, gays, bisexuales, transgénero, intersexuales y queer en el Perú.* Lima: Tránsito—Vías de Comunicación Escénica.

Sosa Villada, Camila. 2016. "Ser travesti es una fiesta, mi amor." *La Tinta*, August 16. latinta.com.ar /2016/08/ser-travesti-es-una-fiesta-mi-amor/.

A Man to Call Your Own

LINO ARRUDA

Abstract This comic was first featured in *Quimer(d)a*, a Brazilian autonomous collaborative comic zine made by travesti/trans* people. In this piece Lino Arruda attempts to address isolation, structural violence, and unintelligibility with humor as he fictionalizes true stories about his experiences coming out as transmasculine in Brazil.

Keywords trans*, travesti, representation, comic, zine

Lino Arruda is a PhD candidate at Universidade Federal de Santa Catarina. He researches monstrosity and animality within travesti/trans* *sudaca* self-representations and collaborates on an autonomous *distro* for archiving, producing, translating, and distributing *kuir* (queer) Latin American zines. His autobiographical graphic novel *Monstrans: Experiencing Horrormones* is forthcoming from Itaú Rumos.

TSQ: Transgender Studies Quarterly ★ Volume 6, Number 2 ★ May 2019   **254**
DOI 10.1215/23289252-7348538   © 2019 Duke University Press

A MAN TO CALL YOUR OWN

even if it's me *!

The hormones have changed me in many ways.

Some more obvious than others.

Before testosterone I never wore bras.

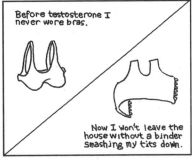

Now I won't leave the house without a binder smashing my tits down.

Before testosterone I only had a tiny piece of broken mirror.

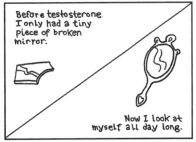

Now I look at myself all day long.

What was OBSOLETE then...

Is now indispensable.

Coconut soap was for a long time my only personal hygiene product.

Kombucha face mask
CLAY
←Ricinus oil
Antibiotic
Sulfur
Aloe
Loofa

Now there is an ever growing arsenal.

*References the song "Um homem pra chamar de seu" by popular Brazilian lesbian singer Marina Lima.

Kiss

SUSY SHOCK

Translated by IAN RUSSELL

Kissing each other in dark corners
kissing each other right in the guard's face
kissing each other at the doors of the Holy Cathedral of Nasty Deeds
kissing each other in the Plaza of every Republic
(or particularly picking out the plazas where they'll still kill you for a Sodom
     and Gomorrah kiss)
kissing each other in front of the photo of the boy I've also been
(and feeling myself wink at myself: keep going, don't stop, don't let it end, because
     that boy likes that kiss . . .)
kissing each other knowing that our saliva drags in tow denied/eclipsed/turned
     off/cut off/mutilated/starving kisses that are not only ours
knowing that your lips and mine while they split the earth they build it
and there's a whole history of kisses that fear stopped from existing
and that's why i kiss you
i kiss them
you kiss me
we will kiss
and that's why i kiss
the kiss

Susy Shock is a trans *sudaca* writer, actress, poet, songwriter, and educator living in Buenos Aires. Her two most recent collections of poetry are titled *Poemario trans pirado* (2011) and *Relatos en canecalón* (2011). She regularly collaborates with a number of cultural magazines, including the *Soy* LGBTQ supplement of the major Argentine newspaper *Página/12*.

Ian Russell is a PhD candidate in Brown University's Department of Hispanic Studies. His work focuses on transatlantic performance and queer temporalities.

TSQ: Transgender Studies Quarterly ∗ Volume 6, Number 2 ∗ May 2019   **259**
DOI 10.1215/23289252-7348552   © 2019 Duke University Press

Living on All Fours

Latinx Performance and the Trans Human Turn in En Cuatro Patas

BERNADINE HERNÁNDEZ

Abstract *En Cuatro Patas*, part of the Pacific Standard Time Festival: Live Art LA/LA and translated as *On All Fours*, redefines the boundaries of the human through the animalistic, arthropod, subhuman, and transhuman. It is curated by Nao Bustamante and Xandra Ibarra, known as La Chica Boom, two artists who utilize ironic avant-garde, spectacle-driven kitsch performance aesthetics in their own right. Bustamante and Ibarra very specifically curated the performances to explore and embody the limits of the human in relation to the Latinx body, which interestingly pushes against and beyond queerness by evoking the prefix *trans* as Latinx transhuman.
Keywords performance art, Latinx, trans human

> We have people coming into the country, or trying to come in—we're stopping
> a lot of them. You wouldn't believe how bad these people are. These aren't people,
> these are animals, and we're taking them out of the country at a level and at a rate
> that's never happened before.
> —Donald Trump, immigration roundtable with California sheriffs, May 16, 2018

On May 21, 2018, the White House released a press statement, or "informational statement," under their Law and Justice category titled "What You Need to Know about the Violent Animals of MS-13," just five days after Trump sat at a roundtable with California sheriffs and vocalized his thoughts about Latinx immigrants. The bulk of the informational statement speaks to how "innocent Americans" have fallen victim to the "unthinkable violence of MS-13's animals" (White House 2018). The rhetoric of the statement falls in line with conventional scare tactics the media tends to utilize without nuance to push certain political agendas. What mostly goes unnoticed in the statement is that all the "facts" of the violent crimes these "animals" commit are not factual statements. Statements

TSQ: Transgender Studies Quarterly ★ Volume 6, Number 2 ★ May 2019
DOI 10.1215/23289252-7348566   © 2019 Duke University Press

such as, "In April 2017, police *believe* four young men were brutally murdered by MS-13 animals on Long Island" (emphasis added) give no concrete evidence, and even with the poorly written White House statement out in the world, one has to wonder, What does it mean to liken an entire population of racialized, immigrant people to animals? As history proves during westward expansion and over again thereafter, this is not the first time Latinx subjects were labeled uncivil and likened to animals. In fact, the language of colonialism from centuries before cemented a language of primitiveness to dark Spanish-speaking peoples and indigenous populations. But what is more important to ask is, Can we ever circumvent the colonial ideological primitiveness of the animal or of the wild? Is there a different political formation to come out of thinking through the subjectivities of the animal?

En Cuatro Patas, part of the Pacific Standard Time Festival: Live Art LA/LA (PST LA/LA) and translated as *On All Fours*, redefines the boundaries of the human through the animalistic, arthropod, subhuman, and transhuman. It is curated by Nao Bustamante and Xandra Ibarra, known as La Chica Boom, two artists who utilize ironic avant-garde, spectacle-driven kitsch performance aesthetics in their own right. Bustamante and Ibarra very specifically curated the performances to explore and embody the limits of the human in relation to the Latinx body, which interestingly pushes against and beyond queerness by evoking the prefix *trans* as Latinx transhuman. Queerness "remains open to a continuing critique of its exclusionary operations" but struggles with, as José Esteban Muñoz (2015: 209) puts it, an "[attempt] to touch inhumanity [and] loses traction and falls back onto the predictable coordinates of a relationality that announces itself as universal, but is, in fact, only a substrata of the various potential interlays of life within which ones is always inculcated." *En Cuatro Patas* obliterates the conception of the human and the ways in which queer theory centralizes gender and nonbinary performativity and transness as metaphor. Moreover, to read *En Cuatro Patas* through the prefix *trans* allows us to link the ways in which Latinx bodies have always been nonhuman through programs like the Bracero Program, which metaphorized the body as just a part of the whole (the representational figure being the arm [*bracero*] of the farm worker) and the ways in which Latinx bodies are mapped as animalistic through the transnational locations of migration and movement. *En Cuatro Patas* examines how brownness conditions the very ways in which the human is constructed and how "the question of race's reality has and continues to bear directly on hierarchies of knowledge pertaining to the nature of reality itself" (Jackson 2015: 216).

This four-part performance series examines how racial and gendered discourse casts Latinx subjects and other mestizo subjects as animalistic, arthropods, subhuman, and transhuman. Part of PST LA/LA, led by the Getty, this unique series is a four-part program that became part of the Broad's programming in 2018 and extended past the PST LA/LA performances. The unique performances explore the disobedient, abject, degraded, and excessive politicized Latinx body and dissolve the boundaries between the animal and the human by exploring what type of desire, enjoyment, pleasure, hope, and future we can find through the nonhuman, subhuman, or transhuman. In an interview, I asked Ibarra how exploring the politicized, abject, bestial, nonhuman, and transhuman nature of the body is linked to Latinx. She responded, "Our curation makes a mess of, celebrates, and toys with the predictable humanist construction of the animal as a contaminating threat to humanity. It asks Latinx artists to show us how the animal—on all fours, hairy, maybe with breasts dangling, bound, pregnant, and maybe undisciplined—manages to transgress or bind what divides the human from animal or Latinx from human."[1] The four-part program began with Naomi Rincón Gallardo's *The Formaldehyde Trip*. The second performance installation blended the ugly, wild, and uncomfortable with the corporeal Latinx body through choreographed movements of (re)gaining uncivility in Uruguayan Brooklyn-based choreographer Luciana Achugar's piece *FEELingpleasuresatisfactioncelebration-holyFORM*. This moving piece paired well with the rest of the second installation, which included Mexican Los Angeles–based experimental vocalist Carmina Escobar and videos by Amapola Prada, Joiri Minaya, Xandra Ibarra and Rob Fatal, Julie Tolentino and Abigail Severance, and Mickey Negron. The third and fourth part of the program will feature performances by Deborah Castillo called *Slapping Power*, Oscar David Alvarez called *"Band" Shirts*, Nadia Granados called *Spilled*, Gina Osterloh called *Shadow Woman*, and Nao Bustamante called *Entregados al Deseo* (*Given over to Want*). However, this essay will focus on the sub- and transhuman in relation to the Latinx body and how the enunciation of *trans* as tied to the animal species marks a provocation in which the line between animal species being and the Anthropocene can be nonexistent while imagining a new future of possibility for Latinx bodies.

Naomi Rincón Gallardo's *The Formaldehyde Trip* is a practice in what Eva Hayward and Jami Weinstein (2015: 200) theorize as the prefixial nature of *trans*: "Across, into, and through: a prepositional force—further [transfigured by] the animal turn" as a "threshold on emergence." Rincón Gallardo, an artist from Mexico City, fuses together songs and videos dedicated to murdered Mixtec activist Alberta "Bety" Cariño and mixes vernacular ideas of speculative fiction with a journey through the underworld. First, the performance lies at the interstices of form and genre, mixing the speculative fiction journey of Bety Cariño through the underworld, who was killed in 2010 in a paramilitary ambush in a humanitarian caravan in San Juan Copala, Oaxaca, with a transtemporal journey where she finds companions with intersexed animals and deities who guide her toward a rebirth ceremony. The cycle of song and video coupled with the ornate animal species costume weaves Mexican B-side sci-fi films of the 1960s and 1970s with Mesoamerican cosmologies, feminist and indigenous activisms, and the Latinx corporeal body (see fig. 1). The Latinx body is always already becoming in this performance piece, which gives the audience the space to imagine what possibilities are ahead for the liminal body that is turned in to different animals and deities throughout the performance.

The transhuman in this piece is not, as Julian Huxley (1957: 17) coined, as "man transcending himself . . . [and] new possibilities" but as "a form of being with distinct capacities for reciprocity with agencies that dominant historiographies struggle to ratify" (Lewis 2017: 206). What we get is the solidification of transhuman with trans embodiment through the inhuman. The Latinx transhuman relates to trans embodiment through the "always becoming" and the construction of the excessive Latinx human. The axolotl (Mexican salamander) is the narrator of the trip and begins the show by stating, "On behalf of a denied wretched majority of speechless and paperless others from the so-called Third World, and other endemic species, I welcome you aboard my Formaldehyde Trip." The friction the narrator/salamander poses in the performance functions not only through the dual capacity the talking animal species poses, through their anthropomorphic qualities, but also through the symbolic meaning of these near extinct amphibians: stunted by neoteny (delaying of physiological development) but also able to regenerate limbs by some sort of fantastical elements, a fitting metaphor for the Latinx body, one that in public discourse is stunted yet excessive and thriving. *The Formaldehyde Trip* asks the audience to imagine what a new subjectivity looks like apart from and through the human and most certainly apart from and through the human as constructed through liberal subjectivity, continental philosophy, and queer theory in general. In a journey toward collaborative social struggle that does not deal with a liberal framework of the immigrant success story, this piece fuses rock music with the "it" of Hayward and Weinstein's (2015: 196) project of a space of the abstract that can only be enacted by particular objects, "a process through which thingness or beingness are constituted." That object, thingness, or beingness rests in the tension not only between the peripheral Latinx subjects and imperialism, white supremacy, and capital but also between the Latinx and indigenous subject that needs to be interrogated. In a song toward the end of the show, a punk melody plays while a video with different "humans" in animal species costumes roll around to a chorus that states,

Figure 1. Naomi Rincón Gallardo, *The Formaldehyde Trip*, the Broad, January 20, 2018.

Shoulder to shoulder
mud, mud, mud
elbow to elbow
mud, mud, mud
bones to ashes.

The lyrics represent a process of mutation, of change, and of rebirth. The mud is the maker of something new in between the body parts that it covers. In the end, this performance piece helps a new subject emerge from the murder of Bety Cariño and asks the audience to consider what it means when an artist sets out to place value on different Latinx aesthetics focused on irreverence, degradation, and pleasure.

Just as in *The Formaldehyde Trip,* Luciana Achugar's choreographed piece *FEELingpleasuresatisfactioncelebrationholyFORM* binds the notion of the wild with the process of healing. The performance choreography of this piece breaks the boundaries of performer and audience as both are entwined with each other on the bottom floor of the Broad. Four women, walking around naked with only hair covering their faces and genitals, break the boundaries of what is a "proper" way to exhibit the Latinx body by coming into their corporeality through loud shouts and grunts that take us close to a postcivilized utopian state (see fig. 2). As Michael Taussig (1987: 132) notes, colonialism entails wildness and violence projected onto things and claims to dictate "civility" when there is always a brutality in its own actions. Achugar's piece allows for the collective to interrogate what it means to "unleash the wild within knowledge production itself" (Halberstam 2014: 121). We begin to ask ourselves, What does it mean to tame a wild animal? Do we only have this notion of "taming" as dialectic to imprisonment? How can the Latinx trans/sub human provide (un)meaning to the signifier of animal? Achugar's piece brings us to question the reality that we live in and how we can begin to resignify representation under imperial and colonial logics. There is no break between the audience and the performer, just as there are blurred boundaries between "human" and "animal," for if we were really standing in a reputable museum, we can bring meaning to the "wild" performance only through our understanding of therianthropy, or shape shifting. The four women, often walking on all four of their limbs, shift the audience into interrogating if the colonial and imperial logic of the wild is really being upended and (re)signified or merely reproduced on the other end of the spectrum. As Latinx bodies are threatened daily with separation, deportation, and loss of life, the material consequence of being wild is the politics of life and death. Just as this US presidency is attempting to rehash and recreate xenophobic and racist practices on the most vulnerable Latinx subjects, Muñoz (2006: 676) reminds us that brownness is

Figure 2. Luciana Achugar, *FEELingpleasuresatisfactioncelebrationholyFORM*, the Broad, May 24, 2018.

performative and therefore finds meaning in the nonsensical. As the performance comes to a close, the four women attempt to put on a pair of jeans without their hands, wiggling on the floor. They utilize the very commodity being made on the border that separates Mexico and the United States to deploy the trope of civility in juxtaposition with the excessive Latinx subject. Taking its cue from Muñoz once again, Achugar's piece then explores a "mode of brownness that is articulated not as a realist of empirical rendering of Latina or migrant experience, but, instead, a theory of brownness as a simultaneously singular/plural sense of the world" (Muñoz 2013). Feeling the brown through the uncertainness of what was actually taking place in reality made the audience think about how their own reality could never understand the latest headline on the Latinx animal/criminal. Interrogating notions of the wild tells the troubles and joys of existing in spaces of alterity.

En Cuatro Patas interrogates how Latinx corporeality can butt up against, transcend, and interweave with the animalistic, arthropod, the subhuman, or the transhuman. It transcends mainstream ideas about the Latinx body and does not work to (re)signify the meaning thrust on Latinx subjectivity but seeks to find the moments of abject opening that create pathways for becoming. The four-part program sets out to clear the meaning of human as already a subjective being but asks the audience to think about the spaces in between, the becoming of Latinx alterities, and the hope that comes from speculative futures of the animal species.

Bernadine Hernández is assistant professor in the Department of English at the University of New Mexico. She specializes in transnational feminism and sexual economies of the US borderlands, along with American literary and visual studies/empire from the mid-nineteenth century to the early twentieth, borderlands theory, Chicana/Latina literature and sexualities, and Latinx performance art. Her articles have appeared in *Comparative Literature and Culture* and *WSQ*, among others.

Note

1.   Xandra Ibarra, interview by the author, Albuquerque, NM, August 14, 2018.

References

Halberstam, Jack. 2014. "Wildness, Loss, and Death." *Social Text*, no. 121: 137–38.

Hayward, Eva, and Jami Weinstein. 2015. "Introduction: Tranimalities in the Age of Trans* Life." *TSQ* 2, no. 2: 195–208.

Huxley, Julian. 1957. "Transhumanism." In *New Bottles for New Wine*, 13–17. London: Chatto and Windus.

Jackson, Zakiyyah Iman. 2015. "Theorizing Queer Inhumanisms: Outer Worlds: The Persistence of Race in Movement 'Beyond the Human.'" *GLQ* 21, nos. 2–3: 215–18.

Lewis, Abram J. 2017. "Trans Animisms." *Journal of Theoretical Humanities* 22, no. 2: 203–15.

Muñoz, José Esteban. 2006. "Feeling Brown, Feeling Down: Latina Affect, the Performativity of Race, and the Depressive Position." *Signs* 31, no. 3: 675–88.

Muñoz, José Esteban. 2013. "2013 Feminist Theory Workshop Keynote Speaker José Esteban Muñoz." Duke University, Durham, NC. YouTube, May 8. www.youtube.com/watch?v=huGN866GnZE.

Muñoz, José Esteban. 2015. "Theorizing Queer Inhumanisms: The Sense of Brownness." *GLQ* 21, nos. 2–3: 209–10.

Taussig, Michael. 1987. *Shamanism, Colonialism, and the Wild Man*. Chicago: University of Chicago Press.

White House. 2018. "What You Need to Know about the Violent Animals of MS-13." May 21. www .whitehouse.gov/articles/need-know-violent-animals-ms-13/.

Oliverio Rodriguez's *The Last Seduction/La Seducción Fatal* (2015–)

Activating the Obvious as Queer Technique

KEMI ADEYEMI

Abstract This review of Oliverio Rodriguez's ongoing series *The Last Seduction/La Seducción Fatal* examines how his images press against European and South American "masters" of painting through explicitly queer and kinky optics. As Rodriguez uses collage techniques to activate the obvious, he creates a suite that theorizes the queerer grounds on which alternate modes of imaging might reflect the broader, more nuanced and quotidian practices of inhabiting bodies marked as other.
Keywords Oliverio Rodriguez, queer, painting

I n *El Rapto*, Darling Shear reclines in a brown, strappy dress atop a ponygirl, her blonde hair cascading over her shoulder and down her back as her left hand rests on the pony's ass next to a ruby-scarlet tail that dips midthigh. This tail, laced to a butt plug inserted for Darling's pleasure/play/domination/raceplay, matches the ponygirl's bra as well as the hair on their head, a color through-line that draws our sight to the black leather blinders they wear to direct their sight forward. It could be that Darling is jumping onto or off of the pony; her toes are pointed as if in midair, her right hand cast upward, and her right hip is cocked as if in between a here and a there. It could also be that she is merely reclined, using the pony's back as a support for such leisurely pursuits as relaxing amidst the muted brown towns that make up the grassy field in the image's background. There is a productive awkwardness to the image that is amplified by the fact that the unretouched, digital images of Darling and her pony are quite obviously imposed on this background, an oil painting: we see everything from the pony's cellulite to the bounce of the lighting kit off of Darling's face, which has not been blotted. So while their images are heightened by virtue of the image's staging and framing, they are just the same grounded by the materiality of their bodies.

TSQ: Transgender Studies Quarterly ★ Volume 6, Number 2 ★ May 2019   **269**
DOI 10.1215/23289252-7348580   © 2019 Duke University Press

El Rapto is emblematic of Oliverio Rodriguez's ongoing series *The Last Seduction/La Seducción Fatal* (2015–), which, in its formal approach to undoubtedly queer and kinky figures, stages a conversation with canonical portrait painting that is at once generatively obvious and decidedly mundane. Rodriguez developed the series in response to the work of nineteenth-century European and Argentinean artists displayed in the 2014–15 exhibition *La Seducción Fatal* at the Museo Nacional de Bellas Artes in Buenos Aires, which focused specifically on erotic art. The collected works of that exhibition are inextricable from painting's relationship to global, colonial projects. Work rendered during colonial expansion played a central, pedagogical role in teaching Europeans how to see and assess value based on plays of light, shadow, and shine, which added to already established, mathematically informed hierarchies of plane, angle, foreground, and background. Eighteenth- and nineteenth-century painting informed developing theories of scientific racism and sexism and contributed to expanding hypotheses of an ever-more seductive exotic other. The South American painters featured in the museum exhibition that Rodriguez draws inspiration from operated within this logic.

To this end and throughout his series, Rodriguez brings photo and collage techniques together in order to self-consciously appropriate the painterly forms of representation defined by these "masters" of painting, replacing the centers of the image with those most dispossessed within the visual lexicon of the West: people of color, low-income people, gender-nonconforming people, people from the Global South, and so on. Here, Rodriguez's *El Rapto* hearkens to the genre of abduction paintings that took license from Greek and Roman myths and that were present in that exhibition. The ponygirl disrupts the historical rendering of the animal figure that has long symbolized the force of masculine violence, energy, desire, and (alleged) erotic power, whereas Darling, in her body and sentiment, upends the genre's effect of stabilizing an idealized white femininity. Where abduction paintings depict the threatening, masculinist, animalistic figures forcibly taking white women, Rodriguez's *El Rapto* shows a figure instead leaning all of her weight onto a consenting pony, expanding the aged narrative of masculine virility and feminine subjection to demonstrate its ties to misogyny, heterosexism, and racism.

The artist does more than simply situate unexpected bodies in settings or holding postures and objects that are historically attached to the forms and functions of gendered whiteness, however; this is not a collection of works that would suggest nonnormative figures accumulate new forms of value simply because they are present. Rodriguez surely insists on a racialized queer optic that centers fat bodies, brown bodies, bodies that do not conform to limiting gender binaries, and the visible tools of kinky sex play. His specific play with the material lines of artifice makes possible a more complex conversation about the limits of a politics invested in reinserting lost, ignored, demonized, and murdered figures into history. *The Last Seduction/La Seducción Fatal*, perhaps literalizing the slash that is central to the title of the series, hones in on distance itself as the tie that binds his figures together, and us to them, focusing on the impossibility and even lack of desire to be incorporated into and thus particularly intelligible to and within a hegemonic frame.

This line of thought is materialized in Rodriguez's simple play with collage. He leaves muted yet lush oil landscapes of the original paintings largely untouched, setting up the stark contrast between the setting and the figures in the foreground, who are rendered through digital photography. Rodriguez makes no attempt to blend the two: the photographs never match the texture or color qualities of the backgrounds against which they are situated. Instead, the sharpened lines of the figures carefully excised from their Photoshop layers sit on top of the matted backgrounds. The juxtaposition of the two images is thereby established not only by the cut of a line but also through the quality of texture between the painterly brushstrokes that establish each background and the crispness of the high-definition photo. In *Salome*, the titular figure is portrayed by a child wearing flip-flops and draped by scarves that could evoke the heavy tapestry in the background were it not for the fact that we can see nearly every fiber of the quotidian, polyester throw blanket and fringed scarf wrapped around the child's waist.

These considerations of texture are extended to the skin of the figures on display. While the paintings Rodriguez references feature supernaturally proportioned, smooth, ivory bodies, his digital images alert us to the lived materiality of skin—dullness, ashy knees, cellulite—in ways that push against historically informed linkages between high gloss and wealth. We do sometimes see hints of those idealized figures who existed in but were cut from the original paintings, as happens with the hand dropping wisps of flowers in the background of *Eros et Psyche*. In the foreground, the figure on the left has an arm draped across the other's shoulders, clutching crumpled cellophane—a white substance in a hand that gestures toward but never fully mimes the original behind them. The shine of the square, golden frame containing the circular image brings out the shine of the directional lighting of the photo shoot, which bounces off the cellophane the figures wear on their chests and is reflected further in the black high-heeled shoes the figure on the right wears. Eros and Psyche are frequently depicted nude or seminude, but Rodriguez puts his figures in black underwear and wraps them in this cheap plastic that can be used in kinky breathplay; where skin glimpsed under a dash of cloth signals the high eroticism of the work Rodriguez references, here the tactility of a see-through material used to both suffocate and be torn off of someone becomes the regime of seduction.

In *La Nina Sorprendida*—an exact replica of Manet that has been flipped, nodding to the photographic history of the negative, and perhaps the strongest image of the series—a figure sits atop red, draped cloth, her back turned slightly toward us as she looks over her right shoulder at us. A somewhat seamless posture is created between her digitized form and the crossed legs of the original, painted figure, their connection points obscured by the white, Moroccan cloth she clutches on her lap and that wraps down and entangles with the shined, white cloth of Manet's original that entwines their legs together. The leather harness that she wears crisscrosses her back and becomes part of the collection of textures that shape the lushness of the original painting and Rodriguez's reimagining. The harness further cuts through the romance of the genre of the nude painting itself, signaling an intentionality that casts doubt on the "surprise" being captured.

Rodriguez is among a diverse group of artists who are mobilizing the vocabularies of painting and portraiture to intervene on the ways that violent, colonial expansion continues to shape who we see and how, conversing with portraiture as a lasting and important field of play with rich possibilities of revaluing black, brown, and queer figures (as happens in the work of Kehinde Wiley and Jordan Casteel). In collaging divergent forms and textures together and doing little to, say, bring together color and tone in order to create the semblance of a unified figure, Rodriguez can be further read as refusing the virtual mandate that people conform to cis-heteronormative standards of body inhabitation. *The Last Seduction/La Seducción Fatal* can also be read as part of the larger, politically valuable effort to reinsert the images and narratives of those who have been violently scrubbed from the archive, on the one hand, or to introduce a semblance of agency for those who may not have consented to have their images reproduced in the first place.

Rodriguez's heightening of the artifice of the complete image ultimately refuses any historical trajectory that would demand resolution or that would result in a mode of visibility attached to political viability. So, even as he converses with the masters, his formal technique refuses the visual iconicity of said mastery—namely, a virtuosic rendering of the human form—which is laced with white supremacist fantasy of the pure. His approach recalls the title of Kerry James Marshall's review, *Mastry*, a play on spelling that signals the forms of technical and conceptual mastery that are engendered within a community but that are not necessarily in ideological conversation with a white ruling class. Following this, *The Last Seduction/La Seducción Fatal* does not seek to become visible within an eroticized genre that has long contributed to the dehumanization of the very bodies Rodriguez images. It instead theorizes the queerer grounds on which alternate modes of imaging might reflect the broader, more nuanced and quotidian practices of inhabiting bodies marked as other. These practices certainly operationalize new media technologies' abilities to smoothly render multiple and seemingly disparate sites and subjects together. In constantly side-stepping the full potential of these technologies, though, Rodriguez refuses the utopian sensibilities that are invested into them. He instead stages scenes that refuse wholly revisionist histories and teleological progress narratives alike, demonstrating the cobbled together *now* as the site where radical queer and trans narratives are actively shaped.

Kemi Adeyemi is assistant professor of gender, women, and sexuality studies at the University of Washington.

Transcending Disciplinary Boundaries

KWAME HOLMES

Black on Both Sides: A Racial History of Trans Identity
C. Riley Snorton
Minneapolis: University of Minnesota Press, 2017. 272 pp.

Early on in *Black on Both Sides: A Racial History of Trans Identity*, C. Riley Snorton tells readers, "*Black on Both Sides* is not a history per se, so much as it is a set of political propositions, theories of history and writerly experiments." (6) I found Snorton's intentional disruption of our assumptions about what constitutes "a history"—a disruption that continues throughout the text—an apt analogy for the book's theoretical interventions. Trans bodies are most vulnerable to violence when they disrupt our (cis) demands that gender presentation and physical sex provide a mutually constitutive mirror for each other. Snorton's pathbreaking book, though, cares little for our comfort and asks us to sit within the paradox produced by any attempt to conceptually and discretely apprehend histories of blackness/transness, categories which, he asserts and documents, represent conditions of possibility rather than static states of being.

Rather than a "history," *Black on Both Sides* is a piece of critical theory that positions blackness and transness as "appositional," or as terms which can refer to one another. For Snorton, the concept of "transitivity" refers to transness as (and here he quotes Claire Colebrook) "a not-yet differentiated singularity from which distinct genders, races[s], species, sexes, and sexualities are generated" and blackness (and here he references Hortense Spillers and the Afropessimism literature) as "a condition of possibility for the modern world" and an articulation of "the paradox of nonbeing, as expressed in its deployment of appositional flesh" (5). Snorton draws significant inspiration from surrealist French philosophy, long concerned with pushing past both the totalizing taxonomy of Marxism and the hyperindividuation (and inevitability) of psychoanalytic theory in order to

TSQ: Transgender Studies Quarterly ★ Volume 6, Number 2 ★ May 2019
DOI 10.1215/23289252-7348594   © 2019 Duke University Press

divine emergent processes for coming to "know" by meditating on the ongoing interrelation between objects (including the subject as object). Or, as Snorton puts it, "Reading 'black' and 'trans' in transitive relations, then, requires that one become acquainted with the social life of things, which is also to consider how one's relationship to things and as a thing entails a confrontation and rethinking of the past as it has been rendered into History" (6). Disinterested in framing black and trans within a mutually constitutive dialectic, Snorton attempts to see what happens when they are brought close, either by the ways in which political and medical elites attempted to deploy gender to racialize blackness or through his own creative intermixture of historical documents.

Brilliantly, Snorton reveals the limitations of the French philosophical project by centering the implications of racial capitalism's demand that blackness be equated with thingness. Inherent to French philosophy's concern with interrelation is the presumption that a universal human, or nonobject, can (and should) attempt to imagine itself as an object (or as a plant capable of photosynthesis, as Gilles Deleuze and Félix Guattari sometimes suggest). Snorton, working from the black feminist theory of Hortense Spillers and Sylvia Wynter, as well as Fanonian phenomenology, illustrates that racial capitalism forced black bodies to *begin* existence as objects. Black subjects need not move to consider their potential thingness. Rather, thingness or fleshness or transness has already been prescribed for them. Black "things" or "flesh" becomes legible, Snorton reveals, via interactions with objects that measure (through medical examination, photography, newspaper investigation, illustration, and personal narrative) and attempt to understand what they are. Spillers's framing of black flesh as fungible helps Snorton reveal that racial capitalism made blackness into a tool within the project of apprehending/making "real" categories of gender. Within this framework, Snorton's book unfolds chronologically, with chapters on nineteenth-century gynecology, slave fugitivity, early twentieth-century black autobiographical and sociological writing, mid-twentieth-century black media, and late twentieth-century black documentary film, respectively.

In his chapter on J. Marion Sims, Snorton presents the speculum as an object that gained meaning as a source of knowledge about the "female body" through violent interactions with enslaved black women who were deemed neither "man" nor "woman" but were medically productive flesh. Similarly, Snorton's chapter on fugitive slaves and fugitive slave narratives reveals that access to emancipation was often conditioned by enslaved people's willingness and ability to make their gender illegible to white observers. Snorton's subsequent chapter on the hidden black maternal figure within Booker T. Washington's *Up from Slavery* and W. E. B. DuBois's *The Souls of Black Folk* and *The Autobiography of an Ex-Colored Man* starts off stronger than it concludes and, ultimately, other readers may more readily connect with the material. Snorton's heterotopic method (and dense writing style) ensures that not all of *Black on Both Sides* will work for everyone. But it is impossible, I think, for even the most theory-averse readers within transgender, feminist, and/or queer studies to entirely dismiss the wealth of provocative insights.

I most positively responded to chapter 4, where Snorton takes the public statements of black drag and trans celebrities (mediated through the midtwentieth-century black press) to think through black people's vexed relationship to national belonging. During the Cold War, black political leaders faced enormous pressure to represent the black body politic as prepared to mimic patriotic anticommunism. Snorton's analysis of black drag and trans celebrities' representational relationship to Christine Jorgensen, herself a symbol of deviance, reveals that black subjects are actually compelled to mimicry itself, rather than normativity. In Snorton's reading, black trans celebrities are forced to narrate their experience through Jorgensen, as a constituent of her experience rather than their own, much in the same way black liberals are forced to mimic American politics, narrating their grievance through Constitutional values. By showing the compulsion to mimicry, Snorton reveals the way drag and trans theories expand our understanding of the workings of racialization.

At times, Snorton's investment in indefiniteness works against his efforts to induce meditative openness in the reader. I found myself unsure about the text's relationship to temporality. As mentioned earlier, Snorton finds great utility in the term "transitivity" as a means of framing blackness and transness as conditions of possibility. Still, a linear conception of time organizes the order of the chapters, which move through the nineteenth, turn of the twentieth, midtwentieth, and late twentieth centuries. This linear organization risks lulling the reader into the belief that there is a historicist project hidden within the disavowal of historicist methods. In light of the text's linearity, can readers be blamed for interpreting statements like "*Black on Both Sides* explains how the condensation of transness into the category of transgender is a racial narrative" (8) as historicist rationales for how that condensation occurred over time? What too is the relationship between blackness/transness as conditions of possibility and Snorton's description of his archive as limited by acts of erasure (itself a linear notion). It is possible "erasure" refers here to random mishandling of materials, but Snorton's description of the problem reads as if historical black trans subjects were identifiable enough to be targeted for removal from the archive. In explaining the historical epochs he works within, Snorton further confounded my sense of his work's relationship to linear temporality by writing "I focus on the transitive connections within blackness and transness that emerge in moments of transition: from slavery to emancipation and the free market, from civil rights to

Black Power movement; from World War II to the Cold War; and from analog to digital" (9). But of course, these moments (with the exception of civil rights to Black Power) only make sense to us as absolute barriers between political, economic, and cultural periods. Perhaps the University of Minnesota Press requested that Snorton chronologically order his chapters in this way, and one gets the sense that they may have strongly suggested the subtitle "*A Racial History of Trans Identity.*" Nonetheless, these aspects of the text encouraged me to ponder the distinction between paradox, which the work openly explores, and the contradictions I observed between some of Snorton's philosophical interventions.

One final connection between Snorton's work and French surrealists is his willingness to transform the text into an illustration of theory. In the same way we should not approach trans people with an eye for understanding their "true" sex, and in the same way we do violence to transness by suggesting there is a moment when transition comes to a discrete end, readers should not approach *Black on Both Sides* with an eye for identifying the work's "true argument" or summarizing "conclusion." Indeed, while the book comes to an end, the work does not offer a concluding chapter. Instead, Snorton's project—much like the ever spinning Bagua or the Sufi mystic's whirling dervish—is an incitement to meditation premised in the unfixed character of reality and consciousness. Readers should expect to leave the text with more, though entirely different, questions than they had at the start. I suspect a range of academics will benefit from embarking on their own journeys with Snorton's scholarship, and I look forward to the debates *Black on Both Sides* will inspire for years to come.

Kwame Holmes is assistant professor of ethnic studies at the University of Colorado Boulder. He is a historian of race, sexuality, and capitalism in the modern city, and his work has appeared in *Radical History Review*, *No Tea No Shade: New Writings in Black Queer Studies*, and *The Routledge History of Queer America*.

The first introductory textbook for transgender/trans studies at the undergraduate level

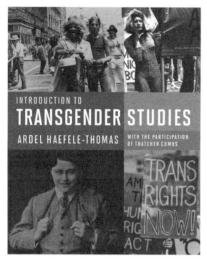

INTRODUCTION TO TRANSGENDER STUDIES

by Ardel Haefele-Thomas, PhD

with the participation of Thatcher Combs

Foreword by Susan Stryker

This is the first introductory textbook intended for courses in transgender/trans studies at the undergraduate level. It can easily be used in LGBTQ, queer, and gender/feminist studies.

Written by an accomplished teacher with experience in a wide variety of higher learning institutions, it explores not only contemporary transgender issues and experiences but also the history of gender diversity around the world.

It encompasses and connects global contexts, intersecting identities, historic and contemporary issues, literature, politics, art, and culture.

Ardel Haefele-Thomas embraces the richness of intersecting identities—how race, ethnicity, sexual orientation, class, nation, religion, and ability have cross-influenced to shape the transgender experience and trans culture across and beyond the binary.

PRAISED BY LEADERS IN TRANSGENDER STUDIES

"Ardel Haefele-Thomas has given the rising generation a generous gift."
—**Susan Stryker,** coeditor of *Transgender Studies Quarterly,* University of Arizona (from the foreword)

"I can't imagine a better textbook introducing students to transgender studies."
—**Paisley Currah,** coeditor of *Transgender Studies Quarterly,* City University of New York

---

USER-FRIENDLY
- written by a trusted authority
- single-authored
- writings from the community
- inviting, attractive, and reader-friendly design

HARRINGTON PARK PRESS
harringtonparkpress.com   NEW YORK CITY

Distributed Internationally by

COLUMBIA UNIVERSITY PRESS